Responses to 101 Questions on the Mass

Responses to 101 Questions on the Mass

Kevin W. Irwin

PAULIST PRESS
New York/Mahwah, N.J.

The Publisher gratefully acknowledges the use of the following. Excerpts from the New American Bible copyright © 1970 Confraternity of Christian Doctrine, Inc., Washington, D.C. Reprinted with permission. All rights reserved. *Guidelines for Receiving Communion* copyright © 1996 United States Catholic Conference, Inc., Washington, D.C. Reprinted with permission. All rights reserved. Excerpts from the English translation of *The Roman Missal* © 1973, International Committee on English in the Liturgy, Inc., (ICEL); excerpts from the English translation of *Documents on the Liturgy, 1963–1979*; *Conciliar Papal and Curial Texts* © 1982, ICEL. All rights reserved. Excerpts from *The Code of Canon Law, Latin-English Edition* (a translation of Codex Iuris Canonici, © Copyright 1983 by Libreria Editrice Vaticana) prepared under the auspices of the Canon Law Society of America, Washington, D.C., 1983. Reprinted with permission of the Canon Law Society of America.

Library of Congress Cataloging-in-Publication Data

Irwin, Kevin W.
    Responses to 101 questions on the Mass / Kevin W. Irwin.
      p.   cm.
      ISBN 0-8091-3888-3 (alk. paper)
      1. Mass Miscellanea. I. Title. II. Title: Responses to one hundred one questions on the Mass. III. Title: Responses to one hundred and one questions on the Mass.
    BX2230.2.I79   1999   99-42604
    264´.02036—dc21   CIP

Published by Paulist Press
997 Macarthur Boulevard
Mahwah, New Jersey 07430

www.paulistpress.com

Printed and bound in the
United States of America

CONTENTS

II. *Liturgical Roles* (Questions 7–16)

III. *Reform of the Liturgy* (Questions 17–23)

IV. *Introductory Rites* (Questions 24–30)

V. *Liturgy of the Word* (Questions 31–44)

VI. *Liturgy of the Eucharist* (Questions 45–66)

VII. *Communion Rite* (Questions 67–82)

IX. *Eucharistic Doctrine and Discipline* (Questions 88–97)

X. *The Eucharist and Daily Life* (Questions 98–101)

Dedication —

to

Edward M. Connors

INTRODUCTION

For a dozen years now I have taught graduate courses at The Catholic University of America on the Eucharist, ordained ministry and ecumenical issues in sacramental theology (among other things) and have been privileged to offer this service to my students and through them to a wider church. At the same time I have been invited to lecture on these same issues at various diocesan convocations, institutes and seminars for a variety of audiences with a broad range of educational and theological backgrounds. Finally, during this same time period I have been in residence in parishes and celebrated Mass daily in a variety of churches in the Washington area. I offer this bit of professional, biographical information in order to provide the lived context from which this book has emerged. The questions I have responded to here have actually been asked of me (although the wording of some of them may be adjusted slightly for greater clarity), and I have tried to respond to them respectfully, fully and clearly. It is a truism in education that you really learn a subject when you are asked to teach it. I judge this to be half of the truth. The other half is that you learn it better when you teach it on different levels and are asked questions from a variety of publics. That way what you might "get away with" in a graduate school seminar simply cannot fly at the end of an adult education lecture in a parish hall. There you can't hide behind jargon (as well informed as it may be!). It is especially there that the "tire hits the road," and the teacher needs to get the point across in clear language with concrete examples. That is what I have striven for here. It is because of these questions (and countless others like them) that I judge that I have become the better teacher, author and preacher. I can attest to the truth of the phrase, "by your pupils you'll be taught." Let this word of introduction be a word of thanks to all of them.

But allow me an additional word about two persons who have helped shaped this book. The first is a former student, Father Chris Beretta, presently teaching at Salesianum High School in Wilmington, Delaware. If I can attest to how students shape me as a teacher, Chris repeatedly asserts what a challenge and real opportunity it is to teach sacraments to high school sophomores. The wording of some of the questions here has been adjusted in light of what he has been asked in the classroom and in light of his invitation that students write down questions they wanted answered about the Mass. I want to thank Chris and his sophomores from the 1998–99 academic year at Salesianum.

Finally, a word about the man to whom I dedicate this book, Monsignor Edward M. Connors of the archdiocese of New York. Here I acknowledge a true mentor and a cherished friend. I have known Ed Connors for over twenty-five years and have only grown in admiration of his gifts as an educational administrator and pastor, not to mention his acumen, wit and wisdom. At Christmas 1992, when I visited with him, he handed me the then recently published book by Raymond Brown entitled *Responses to 101 Questions on the Bible* and asked whether I had read it. I was embarrassed to say that I had not. But, of course, he had! He judged it to be the kind of thing that parishes need for adult education and formation. I immediately borrowed it, digested it and agreed with him. I never thought that some six years later Paulist Press would approach me to add to this series by doing a book on the Mass. Once again, Ed acted as mentor to me and pastor to those whom he thought would be well served by the series, *Responses to 101 Questions on....* It was his encouragement that caused me to write this book.

He is now retired from a permanent assignment in the archdiocese of New York. But he assists regularly by celebrating Masses and preaching as well as continuing numberless informal contacts with fellow priests and lay friends for counsel and advice. My experience of Ed is that he brings a wide-angle lens to church life (especially to problems) and always encourages people to reach beyond their present grasp (to paraphrase Wordsworth) and to be more self-confident. As an administrator and pastor he has encouraged dozens of people to pursue advanced degrees and to offer their gifts to the church. I am one of those to whom he has been mentor. Much of my professional and pastoral life for the past dozen years has been influenced by initial advice he gave me and by our frequent visits and conversations over these years.

This past year has not been kind to him. His health setbacks have caused him to surrender driver's license and car, and to rely on others to help him get about because of his vision and balance problems. In "retirement," he moved from pastoring one of the busiest parishes of the archdiocese to a two-room suite on the top floor of an archdiocesan high school, where he happily shares Eucharist and table fellowship with a number of priest friends and colleagues. This reduction in size of pastoral responsibilities and living space has meant nothing in terms of his breadth, depth, wisdom and wide embrace of so many whom he continues to nurture, advise and encourage. These days it's more common to hear him repeat characteristic phrases such as, "The clock is ticking in each of our lives and you never know whether it's midmorning or five minutes to midnight," or "We come to the Eucharist to receive this presence of Christ now, to this Mass as the hope of heaven." May this book be a modest thank you—a true "eucharist"—to this wise pastor, true mentor and dear friend who has taught me by example how to evaluate what really matters in life as we live it on earth on God's terms and as we yearn for the hope of heaven.

I.

Background and Terminology

1. Where does the term "Mass" come from? Is the Mass the same thing as the sacrament of the Eucharist?

Who am I to debate with Shakespeare's phrase that "A rose by any other name would smell as sweet"? But in fact your question about the names for this sacrament is very important because we use a number of terms to describe it and for a variety of reasons. The short answer is yes, the term "Mass" refers to the sacrament of the Eucharist, where the mystery of our salvation is accomplished (prayer over the gifts, Holy Thursday evening Mass).

Now the term "Mass" itself comes from the Latin text for the dismissal *Ite, missa est*, where the word *missio* means "sending forth." Hence, it literally connotes our being sent forth when the Eucharist has ended to live what we have celebrated. Therefore, one of the options for the dismissal in the present sacramentary for Mass is "go in peace to love and serve the Lord." After the Council of Trent (the church council that met in the sixteenth century to counteract the Reformation) Catholics used the term "Mass" to underscore that central to our faith was the celebration of the Eucharist, our belief in the real presence of Christ in the Eucharist and that at the Eucharist we experience the same sacrifice that Christ endured for our salvation. This was to distinguish us from the Reformers and the subsequent Reformation churches, which emphasized the proclamation of the word to such an extent that they did not emphasize the liturgy of the Lord's Supper and the consecration of bread and wine as the enactment of Christ's sacrifice in this sacrament. (But this statement should not be taken as a sharp division between us today, since in the past thirty years both Catholics and other Christian churches have engaged in the reform of the liturgy to the extent that many other Christian churches celebrate the full Eucharist weekly, and we Catholics have grown in our appreciation of the proclamation of the word at Mass.) That Catholics still use the term "Mass" is clear from the Constitution on the Sacred Liturgy of Vatican II, which refers to the Mass (n. 56) as containing both the Liturgy of the Word and the Liturgy of the Eucharist. This text is found in several post–Vatican II documents to emphasize that today we Catholics want to emphasize both the Word and the Eucharist. But sometimes today the term "Mass" is not used in favor of the expression "the celebration of the Eucharist" or "the liturgy." The reason for this is to emphasize the action of celebrating the Eucharist with the people's participation as central to what occurs. Also, it is helpful to remind ourselves that in Roman Catholicism we use the term "liturgy" to refer to all seven sacraments and other ritual actions of the church, including the Liturgy of the Hours, the dedication of churches, among others. This means that for us the term "liturgy" is much wider than "Eucharist" or "Mass."

Until recently it was common to refer to the celebration of the Eucharist at a wedding as a "Nuptial Mass," from the Latin *nuptiae*, meaning "wedding." More commonly today we would use a phrase such as "the wedding Eucharist." Also, it had been customary to use the term "dry Mass" to refer to a demonstration of the Mass for instructional purposes. More commonly, when this is done today it is more accurately called a "dramatization" of the Mass lest it appear in any way to simulate the actual Mass. However, you find the term "Mass" commonly used today in reference to a "healing Mass" or a "children's Mass." In fact every celebration of the Mass contains aspects of healing, and so the term "healing Mass" is technically redundant. However, the term is pastorally helpful because people will know that the invocation of God's healing grace will be emphasized on these occasions for those physically ill or emotionally disturbed. Some people find these Masses very comforting as they deal with the human tragedies of terminal illness, sexual or emotional abuse and so forth. With regard to children's Masses the Vatican issued a special *Directory for Masses with Children* on the Solemnity of All Saints (November 1) 1973, which indicated when there are a number of adults present that children could be separated from the main assembly for the Liturgy of the Word (chapter 2) or that when there are many children present and fewer adults (chapter 3) some elements of the Mass could be accommodated to their age levels and ability to participate.

There are also several other terms that describe the Eucharist, for example the *Catechism of the Catholic Church* includes "the Lord's Supper," "the Breaking of Bread," the "memorial of the Lord's passion and resurrection," the " holy sacrifice" and " holy communion" (see nn. 1328–32). Each of these carries a connotation that emphasizes one or another aspect of the Eucharist. Hence, to use the term "the Lord's Supper" we are emphasizing the meal aspect of the celebration. When we use the term "holy sacrifice" we emphasize that through this action we experience the very same act of sacrifice Christ accomplished for our salvation.

In summary, I'd say that you will not find the term "Mass" used as much today as formerly but that it still has a place in our church vocabulary (hence the title for this book!). What you will more commonly find today is the term "Eucharist," which emphasizes the Liturgy of the Eucharist and our active participation in both the Word and Lord's Supper.

2. It sounds strange to use the word "celebrate" for such a formal ceremony. What are we supposed to be celebrating?

Your question is extremely important and at the heart of our faith life, which is clearly serious and profound. But it's also joyful and enriching of every aspect of our lives because our faith is in a God of the living who came that we might have life in abundance. The liturgy is formal in the sense that it's a ritual that we follow (and don't make up as we go along). But in essence it's always about the good news of our salvation in Christ and union with one another through him. Let me try to explain this more fully.

There is an important principle that has been used since the fifth century that describes how we can explain the meaning of any part of liturgy. In summary form it asserts that "the law of prayer is the law of belief." Originally it was asserted by Prosper of Aquitaine between 435 and 442 when he commented on the prayers that the church was then using on Good Friday as intercessions. (Perhaps you recall that the structure of the intercessions on Good Friday differs from the structure of this prayer at most Masses. That is, on Good Friday the intention is announced, for example, "for the Jewish people," followed by silence, and then a concluding prayer by the priest.) Prosper commented on the style and structure of these prayers and stated that "the law of prayer establishes the law of belief." From that time to this (including explicit statements in the papal magisterium, e.g., Pope John Paul II) we have looked to what the liturgy says and does as our primary source for understanding what the liturgy is.

We will use this principle over and over in this book, so that what we pray becomes a firm basis for what we believe. One prayer that commentators have used over the centuries (literally!) to describe what we do at Mass is summarized in the sentence from the prayer over the gifts on

Holy Thursday at the evening Mass of the Lord's Supper. I'm sure you know how important this day is in our liturgical calendar—the beginning of the Easter triduum, from Thursday night to Easter Sunday—and also that this prayer is prayed over the gifts on the altar, which are soon to become the body and blood of Christ, a mystery that is especially commemorated on this sacred night. My point is that the placement of this text is no accident and its importance cannot be overestimated. In this prayer we pray:

> *Each time we offer this memorial sacrifice*
> *the work of our redemption is accomplished.*

Let's unpack this phrase by phrase. First of all, the wording of your question and this phrase are extremely important because they both use the plural pronoun *we.* Every time we celebrate the Mass it is always a prayer that *we* pray, for all *our* needs. Even when the priest prays by himself in the liturgy we say that he prays "in the name of the church" *(in persona ecclesiae).* The Mass is not the priest's prayer only; it is the prayer of the whole church, the congregation gathered here and now "in union with the whole church" (as we pray in the Roman canon). Second is the phrase that we *offer this memorial sacrifice.* This explains the central place of the Mass in the whole Christian life. It is unique because through the Mass we experience again and again the very same sacrifice Christ offered for us: his obedient life, humiliation, suffering, death and resurrection. We know that this happened once for all in historical time. We also know that what we do in the liturgy is to experience that same redemption in particular ways here and now. Jesus' one sacrifice has been offered once for all; every time we celebrate the Mass we are drawn into that same sacrifice again and again.

Let's look at another part of the church's prayer to help explain how the liturgy is both the same sacrifice of Christ and our appropriation of it in our need. In Sunday Preface IV we hear:

> By his birth we are reborn.
> In his suffering we are freed from sin.
> By his rising from the dead we rise to everlasting life.
> In his return to you in glory
> we enter into your heavenly kingdom.

All that Christ accomplished for us is offered for us in its fullness, depth and riches in the Mass. Hence, the third important phrase of our Holy Thursday prayer is, *"… the work of our redemption is accomplished."* Notice it does not say it is repeated, or that we do something in addition to what Jesus did. It is the very same sacrificial death and resurrection that we experience through the words, symbols, gestures and actions of the Mass—and we experience this paschal mystery in our need for it and for redemption. Think about why we need redemption: our sense of alienation from God and each other, the sins we have committed and the things we have chosen not to do in our selfishness, the hurts we nurture into grudges, our making idols out of human accomplishments (perhaps even money) as opposed to our real identity and value from God's life and love within us. Once we acknowledge our need for redemption, then the Mass becomes the more and more important as the principal way we experience redemption in our lives.

3. Why are Catholics obliged to attend Sunday Mass? It makes the Mass seem like an unpleasant duty instead of a joyous celebration.

In answering the previous question I emphasized how through the Mass we experience Christ's paschal mystery in a privileged and direct way—and that it was both solemn and joyful. Now this mystery is the heart of our faith. The memorial acclamation in the eucharistic prayer is introduced by the phrase "let us proclaim the mystery of faith." The mystery of our faith, the heart of the matter, is the paschal mystery—Christ's death and resurrection and our dying to sin and rising to real life through him. Because it is the key to all that we believe and because through the Mass we just don't think about it but we truly experience it and participate in it (literally "take part in it"), it makes sense that the church would want to insist on how important it is by making it obligatory. Put a different way: Because it is so important, why wouldn't we want to go at least every Sunday?

Let me move to another level of your question: namely why *Sunday* Mass is so important as opposed to other days of the week. Part of the answer comes from the Jewish origins of what we celebrate liturgically. In accord with the prescriptions of the Mosaic Law, Jews were to "keep holy the sabbath day," which is Saturday for us. This was the seventh day of creation, the day God rested and the day Jews were to remember their passing over from slavery to freedom through the Red Sea. Now if "the seventh day" was so important as the celebration of the covenant God made with the followers of Moses, it makes literal and symbolic sense that the early Christians adopted the next day—the eighth day—as the day when we would celebrate our relationship to God through the new covenant in Christ. But what we also celebrate at Sunday Mass is the breaking in of the new kingdom of God through Christ, what we technically call the eschatological "day of the Lord," the future kingdom in eternity. So Sunday becomes not only a day to look back at what Christ did once in history, it is also a day to look forward to the time when there will be no more need for liturgy (as we sing in the familiar hymn "when sacraments shall cease") and we will sit at the banquet of the Lamb in the kingdom forever. Hence it is quite logical and appropriate that *Sunday* Mass is regarded as qualitatively and theologically more important than the Eucharist we celebrate on any other day. It is the sacrament that defines the church as it journeys to the kingdom of God.

Now I am well aware that there are places where, because of the shortage of ordained priests to serve as pastors, some parishes cannot offer Mass on every Sunday. When this happens the people use a rather new form of Sunday liturgy entitled *"Sunday Worship in the Absence of a Priest."* I'll say more about this later on (especially as I reply to question 5, which is specifically about this rite) but if you read the General Instruction to this rite and what the Vatican and the United States bishops have to say about the situation of "pastorless parishes" what is clear is that because of the nature of Sunday as the key, pivotal day of the liturgical week, that congregations should come together on the Lord's day, even "in the absence of a priest," to deepen its experience of Christ's paschal mystery, even though they cannot always celebrate the Eucharist in its fullness on Sunday.

Time was, of course, that the "Sunday obligation" meant Sunday from midnight to midnight and there was no such thing as the Saturday evening Mass. The basic rationale for extending the Sunday Mass to be celebrated on Saturday evening as well (the parallel is for the obligation of days of precept, otherwise called "holy days," to be satisfied the evening before these feasts) goes back to Judaism and the way its followers "tell time." From the book of Genesis on, the Jews end and begin the day at sunset: "and it was evening and morning the third day...." This was the religious and liturgical background for Christians to celebrate the start of

Sunday at Saturday night Evening Prayer (part of the Liturgy of the Hours) as well as through all the other parts of the Hours and the Eucharist on Sunday. In effect, the liturgical time of any Sunday was always approximately thirty or so hours, not twenty-four, with the Eucharist as its high point. This precedent and the pastoral need to allow people who could not get to Sunday Mass conveniently led to the pastoral judgment to allow Masses on Saturday evenings to be Masses of Sunday for convenience. The intended "audience" for this accommodation were those, for example, who worked irregular hours, in shifts or who lived in places where a priest was available only on Saturday evenings because of Sunday commitments elsewhere. The theory behind the Saturday exception was that it not diminish the theology of Sunday and that it not be frequented regularly. At the same time, however, I think a certain pastoral judgment should both uphold the value of Sunday but also appreciate that Saturday evening Masses can be especially convenient for the elderly who choose to go regularly on Saturdays because by that time of day their limbs cooperate and they can walk and get around easily, or they can avoid the crush and rush of the Sunday morning parking lot issues or because they know they feel "up to it" on Saturday but are not always sure they will feel so well the next day. Lest they then miss Mass on Sunday because they are moving slowly or don't feel that well, they legitimately choose to go on Saturday to avoid guilt. You'll notice I said *guilt*. Clearly Sunday obligation does not oblige one who is ill or infirm from age. They would not be guilty of sin at having not participated in Sunday Mass. For the rest of us, however, it is a matter of grave obligation—and of privilege.

4. If the Mass is the prayer of those who come together, how come it is sometimes offered for special intentions or for people who aren't present?

Every Mass is for all the living and all the dead—what we call the communion of the saints. Phrases such as "in union with the whole church" (Roman canon) and

"remember those who take part in this offering,
those here present and all your people
and all those who seek you with a sincere heart" (fourth eucharistic prayer)

remind us of this truth. The very term "prayer of the faithful" underscores this when (normally) the last two petitions are for the sick and the
dead. It's at that point in the liturgy that we call to mind and heart those
who are dear to us who cannot be present because of illness, old age and
so forth.

The other place in the liturgy when the priest acknowledges
(silently) those whom he would remember in a special way through the
intercession of the Mass was during the pause after "let us pray" at the
opening prayer. Sometimes that is called the Mass intention. Sometimes
a priest may state this at the beginning of the Mass. Strictly speaking
there is no requirement that he do this. In some parishes that person or
need is named in the prayer of the faithful, which I would judge to be its
more proper place. This tradition of naming persons or needs goes far
back in our church and is one way of expressing how the Mass is always
for those who gather and for the whole church. If we belong to the communion of the saints it makes sense to intercede for all the church at
every Mass.

5. I live in a rural parish, and when our priest cannot come for Mass we have a "communion service" led by our deacon. I know this isn't a Mass, but could you tell me what it is?

Depending on your diocese, it may be that a number of parishes
experience the same thing you describe. This is because the number of
ordained priests has declined but the number of Catholics has increased. In
order to provide for the spiritual welfare of communities that cannot have
Sunday Mass every week, the Vatican issued directives in 1988 about what
such a service should look like. This document specified that the community should gather on Sunday for a celebration of the Word of God and
"also its completion, when possible, by eucharistic communion." But note
that the emphasis is on gathering for the Word; communion is separate and
sometimes it is not distributed. Hence the term "communion service" is
really not totally accurate.

The book that your deacon is using is a ritual prepared for the
United States entitled *Sunday Worship in the Absence of a Priest*. He
probably also uses the *Lectionary* for the scripture readings for Sunday.
Now you are quite right that this ceremony is not the same as the Mass,
even though it has many parallels. What it lacks is the presentation of

gifts, the proclamation of the eucharistic prayer and hence the consecration of the bread and wine into the body and blood of Christ. Unfortunately it's not the same thing as the Mass, where we present bread and wine at the presentation of the gifts, consecrate them during the eucharistic prayer, break the bread and pour the consecrated wine at the lamb of God and distribute it during communion. As far back as 1742 Pope Benedict XIV stated that the priest and people should share in the same offering at Mass and that communion should be given from hosts consecrated at that Mass. This principle has been repeated ever since so that what is always preferred is receiving communion at Mass where the bread and wine were consecrated. When this doesn't happen there is a lack of integrity in what we do and what happens is that we separate the act of offering Mass from communion. The same problem exists regarding these services without a priest. Such a service is not a Mass in which we take part in the offering of the Mass and receive communion at the same action. It separates what should not be separated.

Sunday Worship in the Absence of a Priest is the best the church can offer until such time as there will be priests available for Mass every Sunday in every parish. For more background, why not read the General Instruction at the beginning of that ritual book? It's a very clear description of what this is and is not.

6. Can you explain the reason why our parish now celebrates baptisms at Sunday Mass? Does this change the meaning of the Mass?

Allow me to begin by talking a bit about the baptism of children itself, since this frames the past and present practices of the way baptisms occur. I suspect that for many (most?) of us the prevailing understanding of baptism before Vatican II was that by the pouring of water and the proclamation of the baptismal formula, the stain of original sin was removed and those baptized could now inherit the kingdom of heaven. Hence one was to be baptized as soon as possible after birth.

There is nothing really wrong with this theology and it has not been overturned with the new rite for infant baptism after Vatican II. But what has occurred in the revision is the important restoration of a host of other images and meanings about baptism that are reflected in the new rite— among which is the theology that through baptism we become members

of the church. In fact this "ecclesial consciousness," meaning our awareness of being members of one another in God's household, is an important emphasis in all our revised sacramental rituals since Vatican II. (For
example, what was once only called confession is now called rites of
penance and of reconciliation, meaning reconciliation with God and one
another.) That baptism leads to church membership is clear. That's why
the rite for the baptism of infants is now placed in the ritual for Christian
initiation with the understanding that baptism leads us to the central
sacrament of our faith—the Eucharist. We are baptized, and through this
sacrament of initiation we are made members of the church whose unique
identity is celebrated and confirmed in the celebration of Mass. Therefore,
there has always been a clear relationship between baptism and the
Eucharist—which has been restored as a chief element of the present rite
for infant baptism.

It's for this reason that many parishes celebrate baptisms at Sunday
Mass. The General Instruction for the baptism of infants states:

> To bring out the paschal character of baptism, it is recommended
> that the sacrament be celebrated during the Easter Vigil or on
> Sunday, when the Church commemorates the Lord's resurrection.
> On Sunday, baptism may be celebrated even during Mass, so that
> the relationship between baptism and eucharist may be clearly seen;
> but this should not be done too often. (n. 9)

My judgment about that last phrase "not be done too often" reflects
the church's wisdom that the communal celebration of each sacrament
should stand on its own as just that—communal celebrations of the
church's full liturgical life—and that other sacraments or rites should not
always be added to the Mass (e.g., evening prayer, baptisms and so forth).
But when baptisms occur at Mass the relationship of church belonging and
appreciating the Eucharist as a sacrament of initiation are both made clear,
and this is quite appropriate theologically and liturgically.

The frequency of when this occurs varies, depending on numbers
and the parish preparation program. In any event the theology behind this
is ecclesial (church) belonging and welcoming. One way that each of us
can ratify this theology would be to be sure to participate in the Sunday
Eucharist when baptisms occur when we can, and then after Mass go to

meet and greet the parents who have infants baptized, in order to make them feel welcomed into the parish and to the church at large.

Finally a brief comment about your last question: Does this change the Mass? No it doesn't. What the celebration of baptism does is to bring out what is always implied in the Mass—that baptism is to be understood as the sacrament of initiation into the church which celebrates Mass as its center of church belonging and the worship of God.

II.

Liturgical Roles

7. I have always referred to the priest as the celebrant. My friend calls him the presider. Is there a difference?

Your question reminds me of the very first question in this book about names for the Mass and how different names bring out different aspects of the same reality. You speak about your using the term "celebrant." This is a relatively common term in our tradition used to describe the priest's role as leader and the one who acts in liturgy "in the person of Christ" *(in persona Christi)*. In the Middle Ages, for example, the priest's power to consecrate the bread and wine was so important that it diminished emphasis on other liturgical roles, even that of the congregation. But with the emphasis stated repeatedly in the Liturgy Constitution of Vatican II and since, that the assembly is to participate actively and knowingly in the liturgy, it is not surprising that some have questioned whether the term "celebrant" is adequate to describe the priest's role. In a real sense all the baptized "celebrate" the liturgy.

In addition, terminology for the priest's role is not uniform in our official liturgical books. Your friend's use of the term "presider" has official sanction in the General Instruction of the Roman Missal (n. 10) when it speaks of the prayers that only the priest says (the eucharistic prayer, opening prayer, prayer over the gifts, prayer after communion) as "presidential prayers." This term refers to the priest's precise role at these parts of the Mass as speaking in the name of Christ and the church but in such a way that these actions do not diminish the role of the whole assembly in celebrating the liturgy.

I'd say that the difference between "celebrant" and "presider" is that "presider" is more specific to the priest's role and "celebrant" can refer both to the priest and to the whole assembly.

8. If we're all celebrants at Mass, doesn't that mean we're all priests in some way?

Well, yes. Our theological tradition has always insisted that at baptism we are made sharers in the royal priesthood of Christ. This is solidly based on such New Testament texts as 1 Peter 2:9–10: "…you, however, are 'a chosen race, a royal priesthood, a holy nation, a people [God] claims for his own to proclaim the glorious works' of the One who called you from darkness into his marvelous light…," which phrasing is found in Sunday preface I, referring to us as a "chosen race, a royal priesthood, a holy nation, a people set apart."

9. Why, then, do we need a priest at all?

Because our theological tradition has also emphasized the difference between what God makes us through baptism and through ordination. These are not the same realities. Ordination is based on baptism and derives from the theology of being consecrated to God. But it draws out one specific dimension of baptism and consecrates a priest to serve the holy people of God at the altar, in liturgy and as a public witness to Christ the servant of all. The very term "priest" emphasizes the role of the ordained in offering the sacrifice of the Mass for and with all of us. He is not alone, but he bears unique responsibility for the Mass. Ordination places the priest in a particular relationship to the whole church, for and with whom he acts in the Mass. It also places him in relation to all the other ordained in the church—bishop, other priests and deacons—as sacramental representatives of Christ. Also, ordination places the priest in direct relationship to all who have gone before us in succession to the apostles as sources of inspiration and reminders that we always act liturgically in the name of the wider and the whole church, from the apostles down to us. Finally, our tradition insists that ordination carries a permanent and lasting character so that a priest is always to act in the name of Christ when he acts in the liturgy, while at the same time he always acts in the name of the whole church *(in persona ecclesiae)* as Christ's representative. Ordination is more than delegating a person for a function. It changes him in a way that is permanent and lasting—for the sake of the church.

10. Laypeople seem to be taking a bigger role in the Mass. Years ago we didn't have lay readers or eucharistic ministers. Is this because of the priest shortage?

No. As a matter of fact as far back as Justin the Martyr (around 150 or so) we have evidence that readers and deacons functioned at Mass. Then in the early Middle Ages, when priests were sent all over Europe to evangelize and celebrate the liturgy, it became common that the priest assume the roles of reader, deacon and such because it was more efficient and reasonable, and because he was sometimes the only baptized person present! But by the late Middle Ages and as endorsed by the missal that we received after the Council of Trent, the priest himself had to perform all the actions of all the ministers and say all the words of the missal in a "low" Mass. Interestingly, however, at a solemn Mass according to the Tridentine rite, priests dressed as deacon and subdeacon and did the parts of the Mass that were proper to their roles (deacons proclaimed the gospel, subdeacons proclaimed the epistle and both assisted at the altar). So in a sense we did have some differentiation of liturgical roles even in the Tridentine rite.

But it was with Vatican II that we restored liturgical roles to a number of persons—readers, acolytes, deacons and so forth. Eucharistic ministers are a slightly different case. It is true that it was only after Vatican II that we began to use them at Mass, largely because of the increased numbers of persons receiving communion. Their role also extends to what deacons did in the early church—bring communion to those not able to be present at Sunday Mass. Now it is common for both deacons and eucharistic ministers to bring the Eucharist to the homebound, to share the day's scriptures with them and to pray with them.

11. How are lectors and eucharistic ministers chosen? Are they supposed to be exemplary Catholics?

The first criterion is competence. Not everyone has the gift for reading in public or for assisting at Mass with decorum and reverence. These roles should engage people in the liturgy and should serve, not dominate, the Mass. Repeated instructions from the United States bishops about selecting such ministers also insist that they be good Catholics whose lives reflect the sacred duties they undertake. This does not mean that they act "holier than thou"; but it also means that people who live lives that are scandalous should not minister at Mass.

12. What special skills should eucharistic ministers have?

They should know the parts of the Mass—especially the rites of communion—so well that they can carry out their role of distributing the Eucharist with reverence and care for those they serve. They should be able to respond to the aging and the sick who cannot physically join the communion line by going to them. They should also be aware of the rest of the ministers of communion at Mass and "fill in" where necessary. After distribution they should help consume any consecrated wine that remains and should assist with reserving any consecrated bread that remains.

Eucharistic ministers who bring the Eucharist to the homebound should have the ability to make them feel relaxed, should share the proclamation of the word with them and their families, discuss the scriptures with them and lead them in prayer. Also, in reference to the issue I raised (in question 5) regarding worship in the absence of a priest, sometimes eucharistic ministers might be among those designated to lead such services. In these cases they should have special training in leading public prayer.

13. I understand that seminarians are officially installed as acolytes or servers and laypersons are not. Why not?

Let me separate the two parts to your question and explain what "install" means and then who may be installed. In the Middle Ages one who was destined to be ordained a priest was ordained to what were then called minor and major orders. The minor orders were porter, lector, exorcist and acolyte. The major orders were subdiaconate, diaconate and priesthood. What happened to this neat configuration was that in 1972 Pope Paul VI issued a directive (called a *motu proprio,* the title of which is *Ministeria quaedam*) that eliminated the terms "minor orders" and "major orders" and referred to the rite whereby one became an officially designated reader or acolyte as an installation. The reason for this was to emphasize that these were liturgical ministries to be undertaken by laypersons and not ordinations reserved only for those seeking priestly ordination. The specific text of the directive states that "ministries may be assigned to lay Christians; hence they are no longer to be considered as reserved to candidates for the sacrament of orders" (n. III).

However, in this same document Paul VI also asserts that "in accordance with the ancient tradition of the Church, institution to the ministries of reader and acolyte is reserved to men" (n. VII). With the ministry of reader being commonly shared today by both men and women, it is very rare that any layman would be so installed because installation would not be possible for women. In addition, now that the Vatican has ruled that diocesan bishops in the United States may allow women to serve at Mass in their dioceses, it is most unusual to find that a man has been officially installed as an acolyte. The only clear and obvious exceptions to these practices are for those men in training for the priesthood who are now installed as readers and acolytes. In effect this means that for the most part only seminarians are installed to these ministries despite the fact that Paul VI intended installations to include laymen.

14. Why do lay liturgical ministers wear special garb in some parishes, while in other places they wear ordinary clothes?

I'm sure it was a surprise to you the first time you saw a layperson ministering at Mass in special clothing. But there are historical precedents for this. For example in the Tridentine rite every person in the sanctuary wore special liturgical clothing. This meant that the ordained (bishop, priest, deacon and subdeacon) dressed in a number of layers: alb (the white undergarment), cincture (tie around the waist), stole (strip of colored cloth around the neck) and chasuble, dalmatic or tunic (colored garment over the whole body). It also meant that those who served at the altar wore cassocks (black or red loose-fitting, ankle-length robes) and surplices (hip-length white garments worn over cassocks) and that choir members sometimes wore garments similar to those worn by the servers.

In the present Mass, however, the roles of server, reader, eucharistic minister and cantor are often assumed by people who are not ordained, and yet sometimes they wear the alb, which was the clergy's "undergarment." Why? The principal reason why some parishes choose this for their liturgical ministers is the statement in the General Instruction of the Roman Missal that "the vestment common to ministers of every rank is the alb" (n. 298). Originally the alb was what we today call the baptismal garment, the white robe that the newly baptized wore after their immersion in water (or after having water poured on them). From the fourth century this white garment was the external sign of baptismal dignity and of belonging to the church. In the present rites for initiation both adults and children are to wear white garments. This was the origin of the alb (Latin for "white"), the garment one wore when ministering at the liturgy. This became the undergarment for the ordained, whose outer garments drew more attention and were usually much more elaborately designed. The purpose of returning the alb to all liturgical ministers was to remind us that we wear special clothing for special events, that the liturgy is just such an event and that what all liturgical ministers have in common is their baptismal dignity and responsibility.

Some parishes, however, choose not to have any ministers other than the priest and deacon wear special garb. Why? The thinking is that wearing special garb can clericalize us all and seem to recall how only the ordained or those destined for ordination (pre–Vatican II notion of altar servers) could minister at the liturgy. The clear emphasis of Vatican II on the call of all the baptized to holiness and on the concept that liturgical ministry derives from our common baptism, not just ordination, makes this an understandable pastoral judgment. The only difficulty with this practice is that the opposite reaction could occur, that is, to clericalize the ordained even more and set them apart from other liturgical ministers and the parish at large because they are the only ones wearing special clothes. I suppose the pastoral application here is that we should take seriously our ministry to each other at the liturgy and outside the liturgy, and that liturgical ministry never be seen as a special status or privilege, no matter what we wear. The real issue is how what we do liturgically resonates with daily life; hence, having the ordained and the baptized serve at the altar reminds us all of our common baptismal calling, ministry and service to one another.

15. I've heard of parishes where women aren't allowed to be liturgical ministers. Why is that?

From as far back as we have documentary evidence in history only men were permitted to function in liturgical roles at Mass because these roles were viewed as leading men to ordination as priests, and priesthood is reserved for celibate males. This was true across the board in the whole Catholic Church. However, after Vatican II (returning to an older custom of the church) many decisions about liturgical practices are now given to the determination of the bishop of a given diocese. Therefore, when the Vatican recently made the determination that women could act as altar servers, it stated that the decision for this to occur had to come from the local bishop of the diocese. In the vast majority of American dioceses it is now the custom that women can function as readers, eucharistic ministers and (most recently) altar servers. However, in the one or two dioceses that restrict liturgical ministering to men only, the bishops' explanations cite how liturgical ministering classically led to priesthood ordination and that they see the practice of limiting liturgical ministering to men as a way to foster priestly vocations.

16. What is the role of the deacon at Mass?

The General Instruction of the Roman Missal gives the instructions for the deacon's role at Mass (nn. 127–41). In the introductory rites the deacon carries the *Book of the Gospels* and places it on the altar. (If incense is used he assists the priest at this point to incense the altar; he himself incenses the gospel book and helps the priest incense the altar at the preparation of the gifts.) In the Liturgy of the Word he proclaims the gospel and announces the intentions of the general intercessions. Sometimes (given requisite preparation and permission) he may preach the homily. At the presentation of the gifts he prepares the altar, hands the priest the paten with the bread to be consecrated, pours wine and a little water into the chalice and gives it to the priest. At the final doxology at the end of the eucharistic prayer he stands next to the priest holding the chalice until the people have concluded the "Amen." He invites the assembly to exchange the sign of peace, assists in the distribution of communion and takes the communion vessels to the side table and purifies them (either at this point or after Mass). He makes any necessary announcements following the prayer after communion and, after the priest's blessing, dismisses the people (using one of the forms such as "go in the peace of Christ"). Of all his functions at Mass, these two are of special significance because they link the Eucharist with daily life. The reason why the deacon announces the intentions for the general intercessions and makes the announcements at the end of Mass is that his ministry spans both church building and marketplace; it bridges sanctuary and home. In the early church and now with the restored diaconate it is the deacon who knows who is ill, in need of charity and social ministry. It is also he who brings to the community's attention church or social concerns, again as a way to bridge liturgy with the living of the gospel.

III.

REFORM OF THE LITURGY

17. Before Vatican II, the Mass was quieter and more prayerful. Now I have a hard time concentrating on my prayer. Why did they change it?

Let me take the last part of your question first. When the bishops at Vatican II described the kind of revision they wanted for the Mass and all the other liturgical rites of the church, they repeatedly stressed that the revised liturgy was to serve the "full, conscious and active participation" that the liturgy by its nature requires. This phrase (or a variation on it) was used over a dozen times in the Liturgy Constitution. The simple reason was that they were reacting to the Tridentine liturgy, which was usually more quiet and which supported a lot of personal prayer. That's what you recall and obviously miss.

But the Tridentine Mass was not the only Mass that ever existed in the church's history. And like all other kinds of liturgy (taken literally from the Greek term *leiturgia*, meaning "work of the people") it is meant to be a public rite that all of us take part in and share in, not only with our minds and hearts, but also with our voices and our bodies. Much of what we do today by means of participation: singing, using gestures, changing postures and such was actually done in the Tridentine rite, but by other people: the choir, servers and other ministers. What Vatican II did was to restore these actions, postures and gestures to us—the whole assembly gathered for worship. They are ours by tradition and right; now they have been restored for our use. But any act of liturgy should also have its times for personal prayer—its pauses and its silences.

For example, built into the pattern of the present Mass are times when there should be silences for our personal heartfelt prayer: at the introduction of the Mass, before the opening prayer, after each of the readings, after the homily and after communion. This is to allow another level and kind of participation: in silence as well as speaking and gesturing.

But these important external changes are not meant to change your attitude about your need for other times of quiet and prayer. Succinctly put, all liturgy is prayer, but not all prayer is liturgy. In fact

I'd say that in order for the Mass to have its deepest impact on us we will need time for other quiet prayer: to reflect on the scriptures and to encounter God in the deepest recesses of our hearts for intimate conversation. Nor should liturgy be viewed as not having moments of quiet prayer in its structure. I suppose the trick here is not to see the Tridentine Mass and today's Mass as opposites but to strive for "a delicate balance" (to use the title of Edward Albee's play) between vocal and gestural participation on the one hand and silent, quiet reflection at times during the liturgy and certainly outside the liturgy on the other.

18. How can there be a "new Mass"? I thought nothing new could be introduced after the last apostle died.

Your question reflects a keen insight about the limitations of revelation. Yes, with the death of the last eyewitness to what Jesus said and did the mission of Christ's revelation was completed. But at the same time, when it comes to unpacking the meaning of what Jesus said and did, the church has the responsibility in every age to explain that revelation as completely as possible and also to explore new ways for that revelation to be understood, communicated and taught. Hence, we can proudly say that we Catholics are not fundamentalists or literalists, but that what was revealed in Christ is continually experienced and expressed anew in every age.

When it comes to the liturgy of the Mass I want to say two things at the same time. First, it is true that from the earliest evidence we have to the present Roman rite, the structure of the Mass has been the same. Second, however, there has always been a tradition of variety in some parts of the way the liturgy was celebrated. You most likely have heard the term "the new Mass"; this is a translation of the Latin term *ordo Missae*, the order of the Mass, with the adjective *novus* referring to the rite of the Mass replacing that from Trent (often called the Tridentine Mass).

With regard to structure, it is clear from the time of Justin the Martyr (150) that the Mass has been composed of the proclamation of the scriptures and the proclamation of the eucharistic prayer, during which the gifts are transformed and the act of receiving communion takes place. Over the centuries, however, this same skeletal structure has been embellished in a number of ways and for a good many reasons. For example, once the Liturgy of the Eucharist was celebrated in the basilicas of the city of Rome, beginning in the fourth century, then the need arose for processions to be added to the proclamation of the scriptures and the action at the altar. Thus, added to the simple structure of Justin the Martyr were processions at the entrance, at the presentation of gifts and at communion, and these ritual actions were accompanied by music. These musical compositions were originally parts of the psalms or other inspired texts, set to music for all to sing. The technical terms for these times for singing were the "introit," the "offertory" and the communion processions. Unfortunately, very often from the Middle Ages on, these texts were either sung by a choir or recited by the priest to himself. They were rarely sung by the whole congregation. It was not a surprise, therefore, that in the 1940s in Europe the more popular form of participation was to sing hymns at these parts of the liturgy even though the priest still recited the Latin antiphons (i.e., the texts set to music to accompany the processions at the introit, offertory and communion) to himself.

An even clearer example of the way the same skeletal structure of the Mass was adapted to different circumstances was the fact that when the Tridentine missal was established as the norm for the whole church from the sixteenth century onward, the provision was also made for those religious communities and some dioceses with their own "rites" of the Mass to keep to those practices and not conform jot and tittle with the then new Tridentine Mass. So, for example, before Vatican II, Dominican priests used their own rite for the Mass, in which the priest placed the wine and water in the chalice at the beginning of the Mass and said very short prayers at the foot of the altar and at the offertory. Similarly, as another example, the diocese of Milan was allowed to keep its own Mass structure, which included an additional prayer of the priest at the presentation of the gifts. Today, the element of the Eucharist that differs most from place to place and from religious community to religious community is the saints commemorated at the liturgy. There is a list of Franciscan, Dominican and Benedictine saints, for example, honored in their communities but not by the universal church. In the same way we American Catholics honor saints who have particular meaning for us but who are not necessarily honored in the rest of the world, such as St. Elizabeth Ann Seton (Jan. 4) and St. John Neuman (Jan. 5).

19. In the old days the priest always spoke the words from the missal. Now some priests seem to go beyond the book and add their own words. Is this permissible?

One of the features of the present Mass is that it gives priests several opportunities to offer comments that are not printed in the missal. For example, at the beginning of the Mass he can choose to briefly introduce the liturgy in his own words. If he uses the third form of the present penitential rite, he can alter the acclamations he addresses to Christ (instead of saying "you came to heal the contrite" he could use another phrase such as "you are the Lamb of God who takes away our sins"). He can make a comment to introduce the scriptures as well as to introduce the preface and eucharistic prayer. He can adjust the introduction to the Lord's Prayer and the words of the dismissal.

In addition to this there are several places in the Mass when he can choose from options given in the present sacramentary. These include the structure of the penitential rite itself (see questions 28 and 29), the choice of the opening prayer on Sunday (from two options) or even the whole set of "presidential prayers" (opening prayer, prayer over the gifts, prayer after communion) on weekdays that have no special feast or that are not in a special season (like Advent, Christmas, Lent or Easter). One of the distinguishing characteristics of the Roman rite, as opposed to the liturgical traditions from the East, for example, is the variety of prefaces (they now number over ninety!) and eucharistic prayers themselves (they now number ten) that can be used at Mass.

20. Are Masses in Latin still allowed?

Yes. You will recall that in answer to question 18 I made a distinction between the present rite of Mass in Latin (called the *novus Ordo Missae*) and the Tridentine Mass in Latin. With regard to the new order of Mass, the clearest statement from Rome about a Latin Mass according to the revision mandated by the Vatican states that "once the vernacular has been introduced into the Mass, local Ordinaries [i.e., bishops of dioceses] should determine whether it is advisable to retain one or more Masses in Latin, particularly sung Masses. This applies especially to great cities in churches with a large attendance of faithful using foreign languages" (n. 48). In 1984 Pope John Paul II granted permission for diocesan bishops to authorize the Tridentine rite to be celebrated in their dioceses under very carefully defined circumstances. Not all bishops authorize these Masses, and where they do, these Masses are not to take away from the authority of the new missal of Pope Paul VI.

The issue of the Latin language does arise rather frequently in descriptions of music to be used at Mass, with the caution lest some of the great treasures of music written for the Mass in Latin be lost. Also, in some musical guidelines support is given for singing some of the parts of the Mass in Latin as a sign of the church's universality throughout the world.

21. What happened to the terms "low," "high" and "solemn high" Mass? Do we still have them?

These terms delineated levels of solemnity and strict rubrical directives in the Tridentine missal. Specifically, they referred to who were the ministers of the Mass, the amount of music to be sung and by whom. This terminology and the strict set of distinctions it reflected in the celebration of Mass were collapsed in favor of the present missal, which allows greater flexibility in the way solemnity is given to various parts of the Mass. For example, in the former "low Mass" nothing was sung, whereas the present missal envisions some singing at every Mass (such as the acclamations at the gospel and during the eucharistic prayer). The term "progressive solemnity" was coined in the General Instruction of the Liturgy of the Hours (n. 273) to indicate that the extreme separation between a choral office and the recited office should be overcome; it further states that decisions regarding flexibility and variety (which parts of the Hours should be sung and on what occasions) should be made by competent persons, depending on pastoral circumstances, ability of the participants and other pastoral need. The same principle can be used regarding what parts of the Mass should be sung, when and by whom. This would mean a shift from the fixity of the former terminology toward greater flexibility. This would accord with the present reform of the Mass, respecting each Mass as the unique experience of Christ's saving mysteries, while still moving within the calendrical rhythm that balances certain special feasts with "ordinary time," as reflected in the way parts of the Mass are executed. For example, on Easter Sunday morning it might be

desirable to have an elaborate gospel procession accompanied by sung
alleluias and to have the gospel itself sung, as opposed to a simpler, sung
gospel acclamation and proclaimed gospel, which is the standard practice
on Sundays of the year.

22. Why was the altar rail removed from the church?

Allow me to begin by offering a bit of background about where
the idea of an altar rail came from. Essentially what occurred in the evolution of church architecture (especially in the Middle Ages) was the
construction of a permanent wall or screen of varying heights that effec-
tively separated what occurred in the sanctuary area from what happened in the nave, or the area where the congregation was located. The
idea was to mark off the sanctuary as the place where the ordained carried on the liturgy on behalf of the congregation. In Italy, for example,
evidences from the early medieval period offer examples of such walls
of up to about three feet to surround the choir area and the ambos (or
pulpits), from which the scriptures were read. By the fifteenth century
in places such as Amiens, Chartres and York, what was constructed
were much higher "screens" whose purpose was to separate the choir
from the nave. So, for example, if you have seen or visited Westminster
Abbey in London and participated in evensong (sung evening prayer)
you may have noticed that some participants assembled inside the sanctuary area with the choir while the majority of other participants were
located outside the sanctuary, separated from the nave by a screen.
When such screens had a cross placed on them they were then called
rood screens, deriving from the old English term *rood* meaning "wood"
(hence our acclamation on Good Friday at the veneration of the cross,
"behold the wood of the cross..."). In effect, any kind of rood screen or
similar structures separated the people from the chancel or sanctuary.

Altar rails came to take their place in Catholic churches, even
though some screens remain in a few Catholic churches. More commonly, what were constructed were railings of varying materials (stone,
wood, iron and so forth) about three feet in height with a gate (or gates)
to allow the entrance of the ordained and other ministers to the sanctuary from the nave side of the church. This occurred at solemn Mass. For
low Mass the ministers entered the sanctuary from the sacristy and
returned to it after Mass without walking through the nave.

A number of theological reasons and symbolic explanations have arisen to explain the altar rail. Suffice it to say that the notion of separation of the people from what occurred at the altar in the sanctuary is chief among the most cogent reasons given. This would also have been supported by much medieval eucharistic liturgy, in which the people were separated from the action of the liturgy and did not receive communion frequently.

The altar rail also functioned at Mass from the medieval period to modern times as the place where communicants would kneel for communion. It should be recalled that kneeling became customary as the posture for the congregation to assume when receiving communion from the thirteenth century onward. Hence the rail was a convenient place to kneel to receive the consecrated host.

In the revision of the liturgy after Vatican II no prescription is made for altar rails in church design or sanctuary decor. The Constitution on the Sacred Liturgy leaves it to territorial bodies of bishops to specify what is required for the altar and other material elements used at Mass (n. 128). The General Instruction of the Roman Missal states that "the main altar should preferably be freestanding, to permit walking around it and celebration facing the people. Its location in the place of worship should be truly central so that the attention of the whole congregation naturally focuses there. Choice of materials for the construction and adornment of the altar is to respect the prescriptions of law. The sanctuary area is to be spacious enough to accommodate the sacred rites" (n. 91).

What is notable here is the concern that what occurs at the altar is able to be seen by the congregation. Therefore any kind of (rood) screen, wall or altar rail separating nave and sanctuary is not envisioned. Clearly a major reason why an altar rail is no longer needed is that we now receive communion while standing, and that it is most often distributed under both forms, necessitating the people to process both to the minister of the eucharistic bread *and* the eucharistic cup. The absence of the altar rail makes the communion procession possible.

The way the sanctuary area is delineated today is most often by having it raised above floor height by a step or a few steps. This allows for visibility, which in turn facilitates participation in the Mass.

23. The Catholic Church I grew up in had many stained-glass windows and statues, but our new parish church doesn't. Why not?

Your question raises some important issues related to the history of art in churches, namely, the relationship of art to the instruction and formation of Christians and, further, the demands that the new liturgy places on artists and pastors in terms of what should be emphasized in redesigning and building churches. Let's take them one at a time.

One of the distinguishing characteristics of Catholicism has been its concern that the arts be utilized and artists supported in the building of beautiful churches for the glory of God. Human ingenuity and creativity are prized because they reflect the donation of the genius and instincts of the human person to create what is true, good and beautiful to reflect the glory of God. The creation of accommodating, inspiring and beautiful churches has been one of Catholicism's chief legacies to the history of Western civilization. For example, think about the number of people who tour the cathedral towns of Europe or who travel to the city of Rome to be inspired by the religious history of those places captured in buildings that reflect God's glory and the achievement of the human spirit. Stained glass is one genre by which artists meticulously created images in such church windows—images that reflected saving history, the deeds of particular saints and other such memorable high points of our religious tradition. It can be said that along with mosaics and sculpture, stained glass was a major vehicle for instruction and formation of adult believers. This leads to my second point.

The cathedral of Chartres in France, for example, is often regarded as a model in the way statuary and stained glass were used to instruct medieval Christians about the faith. Among the hundreds of statues on the facade of the cathedral, the image of Abraham sacrificing Isaac stands as an outstanding image whose beauty deserves attention and reverence. But the statue also instructs! It tell us that Abraham's sacrifice of Isaac prefigured God the Father's allowing his Son, Christ, to be sacrificed for our salvation. This important parallel is reflected in the text of the Roman canon, which refers to "the sacrifice of Abraham our father in faith." But this was likely not heard by Catholics in the medieval period because Mass was in Latin and the canon was said silently. Hence the statuary imaged what the texts said and enabled those who did not comprehend this theology from the texts of the liturgy to appreciate it through this sculpture. Those who instructed adults in the faith could point to Abraham's statue and draw from it the theology of the canon and develop implications for our lives, chief among which would be *obedience* to God's will. Where Adam and Eve *disobeyed*, Abraham's *obedience* was a credit to him, and he was justified before God.

The same thing happened with the stained glass at Chartres. Among the main windows in this cathedral, one is called the Easter window, containing more than thirty smaller windows that tell the story of Jesus' death and resurrection. It begins with the prediction of the passion and the requirement that we carry our cross, to the postresurrection meals with the risen Christ. One of these is the supper of the disciples at Emmaus. Again, a skilled teacher could use this series of windows to "tell the story" of our faith and redemption. What occurs at Mass every time we celebrate it is our taking part in the very dying and rising of Christ through the sacred meal of the Eucharist. Even if this were not so evident in the medieval liturgy of the Mass, it was certainly one of the lessons to be drawn from the artistically beautiful and theologically rich stained glass at Chartres.

Now, to my final point—and really the point of your question— why don't we have the same kind of windows today? There is certainly nothing against them. Think about shrines and cathedrals in our own country and the statuary and stained glass they contain. In the city where I live, Washington, D.C., I often take guests to the Basilica of the National Shrine of the Immaculate Conception on the campus of Catholic University and try to explain the statuary and stained glass of that church and the meaning of the mosaics in the upper and lower churches. It often fascinates and invites them to deeper faith—all through the genius of artists and craftspersons.

But all of this is to be read now in the light of the revised liturgy, where active participation is a chief value and emphasis is placed on all that we do in enacting the liturgy itself. The restoration of the use of a special *chair* from which the priest presides, the restoration of the *ambo* or pulpit for the proclamation of the scriptures and the importance of a free-standing *altar* for the eucharistic action all call out for artists to give special attention to how these are designed within the church as centers of attention and special focus during the liturgy itself. The key here is to see that what is now used in the liturgy is to be designed in such a way that these things are substantial and beautiful, yet functional for the requirements of the liturgy. Therefore, the monies and creativity expended on these elements of the liturgy likely take precedence over stained glass and statuary. My own suspicion is that today, three decades after the revision of the liturgy, we are revisiting something of an imbalance in the direction of the merely functional elements of our churches that serve the new liturgy. We are now in a position to design both what is used in liturgy and what reflects it and other aspects of our faith in other artistic media so that they are truly substantial, evocative of God's glory and helpful toward shaping a liturgy that is participated in and also lived in daily life. I think you will be seeing greater attention in the future to the way the arts can enhance the liturgy and the way both liturgy and the arts are seen to reflect the glory of God.

IV.

INTRODUCTORY RITES

24. When I come into church, I like to be greeted and to say hello to my friends, but in some churches people slip in quietly and don't talk. Is there an ideal way for people to gather for Mass?

I'd say that the ideal way to gather for Mass is to do both. Certainly in the former Tridentine Mass there was an emphasis on silence and reverence before and during the Mass. But even then there were ushers who greeted us, helped us to our pews and facilitated the procession to communion (not to mention taking up the collection!). Today many parishes have a group called ministers of hospitality, who greet us, help us with seating, facilitate the procession with the gifts, direct communion lines and so forth. But certainly today there is legitimate emphasis on what it means to come together as a community of faith for Mass, and this includes greeting other people. The General Instruction of the Roman Missal states that "the purpose of these rites is that the faithful coming together take on the form of a community and prepare themselves to listen to God's word and celebrate the eucharist properly" (n. 24). On the basis of this statement I would say that greeting others before Mass is a way to solidify a sense of community and common purpose in our gathering to celebrate the Mass. At the same time I would also recommend that we use some time before Mass begins and then during the introductory rites to be silent and deepen our awareness of what we are undertaking as a community of God's faithful.

25. The entrance procession seems to exalt the priest. Wouldn't it be better to have him sit somewhere in the church and walk up quietly to the altar to begin the Mass?

Part of my answer is historical and part is theological. First, when the Christian church was first allowed to celebrate liturgy publicly and was recognized as a legitimate religion in the Roman Empire (this is commonly associated with the Edict of Milan in 313), the numbers of Christians grew and the places needed for worship had to be larger. It was at this time that Christianity took over the Roman basilicas and made them houses for worship. These long, normally rectangular buildings required a series of processions: the entrance of priest and ministers, the procession of gifts to the altar, the procession of the faithful at communion time and the recessional at the end of the liturgy. These processions were also accompanied by music and still are to this day: at the entrance (formerly called the introit), at the presentation of gifts (sometimes called the offertory) and at communion time. The functional purpose of the entrance procession is to have the ministers in place for Mass. But the theological reason for the entrance procession and the procession at the end of Mass (recessional) is to signify what all of us do when we celebrate Mass—we gather for worship and are sent forth from worship. We gather in order to disperse to live what we have celebrated.

One thing that might help relieve the impression that the procession is only about the priest is to review the suggested list of who should be in the procession and see to it that these people all participate in the procession with the priest: server with censer (if incense is used), cross and candle bearers, acolytes and other ministers, reader, deacon and priest (General Instruction, n. 82). Another thing to do is to understand why the ministers bow to the altar and why the priest and deacon kiss it. The emphasis in the procession is on the altar, the enduring symbol of Christ, whose sacrificial death and resurrection will be commemorated on it once more. From the time of St. Ambrose on (fifth century), this act of kissing the altar was seen to emphasize the centrality of Christ in what we do liturgically and the symbolism of the altar as connoting the sacrificial aspect of the Mass.

26. Is the book of readings always a part of the entrance procession? Why?

The short answer to your question is that the *Book of the Gospels* (not all the scripture readings, but I'll treat that below) is to be carried by the deacon or the reader. The better answer, however, is to explain what the liturgical instructions say and why, and then to offer a comment on where your question came from. The General Instruction of the Roman Missal states that a reader joins the priest and other ministers in the entrance procession to the altar and that s/he "may carry the *Book of the Gospels*" (n. 82 d). It also indicates that the *Book of the Gospels* is placed on the altar when the ministers reach it in procession (n. 84) and that the priest takes it from the altar during the singing of the alleluia before the gospel is proclaimed. Now we need to remember that this document was originally written in 1970, and at that time the diaconate was not restored as a permanent church ministry. When the *Ceremonial of Bishops* was published in 1984 it was common by then to have deacons ministering at the liturgy, and the norms in the bishops' ceremonial presumed the presence of deacons. Hence it states that at the "stational Mass of the diocesan bishop" the deacon carries the *Book of the Gospels* (n. 128), that he proclaims the gospel at the ambo and, after the bishop, kisses the book (this is the preferred usage but the deacon may kiss it himself). Then the "gospel book is taken to a side table or some other suitable place" (n.141). What happened in the earliest days of the present liturgical reform in the United States was that we didn't have a *Book of the Gospels*; we only had a *Lectionary*, which contained *all* the scripture readings for Mass, not just the gospels. So what happened often in parish celebration in light of the 1970 General Instruction of the Roman Missal, the absence of deacons and no gospel book was that readers commonly carried the *Lectionary* in procession, placed it on the altar or the ambo (a term meaning a raised platform in early Christian basilicas from which the scriptures were proclaimed) and then proclaimed the readings from the ambo. What would be pastorally helpful today would be to place the *Lectionary* at the ambo before Mass begins, to have the readers proclaim the scriptures other than the gospel from the *Lectionary* and then have the deacon (or priest in the deacon's absence) process with the gospel book from the altar to the ambo to proclaim the gospel.

The use of two books for the proclamation of the scriptures should not be interpreted as a separation between the Old Testament and the epistles on the one hand (from the *Lectionary*) and the gospel (from the *Book of the Gospels*) on the other. There is one revealed Word of God in both testaments, but clearly the words of Jesus in the gospels have classically received greater reverence in the church's liturgy. In addition, the use of two specially crafted and designed books can help us appreciate the symbolic value of the proclamation of the word—from beautiful books, not sheets of paper, worship aids or anything of the sort.

27. Why does the priest go to the chair for the beginning of Mass and not the altar?

I've spent a lot of time talking about what the liturgical rites and texts say to discover their theological meanings. Now I have the chance to shift to interpreting what we mean theologically by the placement and use of the chair, a relatively recent addition to the arrangement of our sanctuaries. The theological meaning of the chair as an important place from which the priest presides at Mass derives from the *cathedra* or the bishop's chair in his diocese, which is housed in the central church of the diocese, the cathedral. The cathedra or chair symbolizes both the teaching authority of the bishop and the bishop's communion with the pope and all the bishops in the church. (Hence the great importance attached to a papal teaching *ex cathedra*, literally "from the chair.")

In the reform of the Mass the chair was reintroduced for use at all Masses, whereas in the Tridentine solemn high Mass you may remember that the priests used a side bench when they weren't at the altar. So the regular use of the chair is not new; it's a restoration to an older practice that we now use regularly. The reasoning behind its use is to differentiate the parts of the Mass by location, not just description. According to all post–Vatican II statements about the Mass, its two essential parts are the Liturgy of the Word and the Liturgy of the Eucharist, which are so closely connected as to be one act of worship. Now the priest may preach the homily from the chair, as a symbol of teaching authority. But more commonly in America he chooses to stand at the ambo, as most people do when delivering speeches. More common (and even required!) is the use of the chair when the priest leads the introductory and concluding rites of the Mass. He returns to the chair after the homily to lead the profession of faith and introduce and conclude the intercessions. This location differentiates these parts of the Mass from the primary and truly essential parts: the Word proclaimed from the ambo and the Eucharist from the altar table.

28. The Mass always starts joyfully with song and prayer, but then we move to a somber penitential rite. Why the sudden change?

This is a frequently asked question and an issue that causes some confusion. The General Instruction (n. 24) states that the penitential rite is one element of the "introductory rites," which are "the entrance song, greeting, penitential rite, *Kyrie*, *Gloria*, and opening prayer or collect [which together] have the character of a beginning, introduction, and preparation." Then it goes on to say that "the purpose of these rites is that the faithful coming together take on the form of a community and prepare themselves to listen to God's word and celebrate the eucharist properly." About the penitential rite specifically, the General Instruction of the Roman Missal states that "the priest invites [the congregation] to take part in the penitential rite, which the entire community carries out through a communal confession and which the priest's absolution brings to an end" (n. 29). I suspect from your question that the key word in this description is "confession," since the penitential rite does acknowledge our sinfulness and unworthiness before God, especially through such phrases as "I have sinned through my own fault" in the "I confess" prayer. But the word "confess" also means to declare our faith publicly, and the church sometimes calls certain people "confessors" because they did this in an extraordinary way. So even when we acknowledge our sins, it is with a sense of expressing our faith in God and our thanks to God for forgiveness.

Structurally it is also important to see that in the present form of the penitential rites there are three options (the other option, the blessing with holy water, is discussed in the next question). Each of these is introduced by the priest. *The Sacramentary* contains three choices for suggested wordings at this point of the Mass, but he may also use "these or similar words." In essence, these suggestions invite the assembly to acknowledge their "failures" and "sins" and also to "ask the Lord for pardon and strength" or "the Father's forgiveness for he is full of gentleness and compassion." Here the principle is established of admitting sinfulness in the light of God's forgiving and reconciling love. The first choice that follows is the traditional "I confess" prayer, which has been adjusted in the present *Sacramentary* to read, "in what I have done and in what I have failed to do." Hence it couples admission of sin before God with an admission of our sinfulness in not responding to the needs of others. The second option is a variation on the "Lord have mercy" litany, from the Greek *Kyrie eleison*. In fact, the sense of the original Greek here is not that we strike our breasts and act as though we are "sinners in the hands of an angry God." Rather the sense of the Greek is an acclamation proclaiming God as the ever merciful God on whom we can rely and whose allegiance we profess at the Eucharist. The last option, the rather familiar threefold statements regarding the attributes and names for Christ, is most important theologically because through it we profess faith in who Christ is and what he now does for us at the liturgy. In no way are they statements about what we have done wrong. The priest may use other acclamations should he choose, but always these are to be attributes and names for Christ, who forgives us our sins.

From this evidence of background and present texts in the *Sacramentary* I'd reply that while the penitential rite is part of the introduction to the Mass it should not be understood as overly negative and focused only on sin. It is a communal action whereby we admit our need for God's grace through his Son at the Eucharist we celebrate. Our admission of sin is clearly personal but also done with others who are equally human, fallible and who fall into sin. If we think that the penitential rite is becoming too narrowly focused on our individual sins or on guilt, check the *Sacramentary* and see whether what you are hearing is what is there, either literally or in the spirit of "these or similar words."

29. Why at some Masses do we renew our baptismal vows?

I'm sure you have noticed that traditionally the Catholic Church has placed holy water fonts at the church entrances and that baptisteries were near the rear doors of the church (to signify admission into the community of the baptized). Given the present reform of the liturgy, the baptismal fonts have often been moved to a place of great prominence (normally near the church door), and people are now encouraged to bless themselves not only from holy water fonts but from the baptismal font itself. The theological meaning of this is clear: every Eucharist is a commemoration and a renewal of the covenant of baptism.

It was because this was only done at high Masses in the Tridentine rite that the church began using holy water fonts: so that people could bless themselves whenever they entered the church to signify the connection between baptism and Eucharist. However, with the present reformed eucharistic liturgy, we now have the option of using the "rite of blessing and sprinkling with holy water" as part of the introductory rites at Sunday Mass. We should pay close attention to this prayer because it gives us a brief overview of salvation history and our sharing in God's eternal salvation through the sacred signs of water at baptism and bread and wine at the Eucharist. On Sundays, the day of Christ's rising to new life after his death on the cross, this is clearly a preferable option with which to begin the Eucharist, because it signifies how Sunday Eucharist is the premier liturgical action whereby we renew our baptismal covenant and deepen our conversion to Christ.

In the Tridentine rite this was known as the *asperges me* rite ("you will sprinkle water upon me"), which phrase is from the psalm that was traditionally used to accompany the sprinkling itself (Ps 50:9). In the present reform this same psalm can be used, as can "another antiphon or appropriate song." The theological point here is that through the symbol of water, the texts of the introduction and the blessing prayer, the act of sprinkling and the singing of an appropriate antiphon, we renew our baptismal commitment both at the beginning of the Eucharist and through the whole Eucharist itself.

30. They used to call the opening prayer the collect, to signify that all our intentions were "collected." Why did they change that prayer?

The General Instruction of the Roman Missal still uses the term "collect" along with "opening prayer" and states that "the priest then says the opening prayer, which custom has named the 'collect'" (n. 32). You are quite correct that the term "collect" was often used to signify that moment in the Mass when we would form our intentions for the Mass (call to mind our needs and hopes). Actually this is what should happen after the pause when the priest says "let us pray" before he says the prayer. These pauses are helpful to underscore how the Mass is both communal and public and an act we participate in that also contains some times for personal reflection and prayer.

Now history reveals some interesting background to this notion of "collect." Part of the liturgy in the city of Rome (which also extended to other large cities and dioceses) on special feasts and seasons included "station Masses," when the pope would travel to various churches in Rome for Mass. During Lent this custom included a procession from a gathering place (most often a church) to the church where the Mass was to be celebrated, during which the faithful would join in a penitential procession behind a relic of the true cross. At the time they gathered for the procession a prayer would be prayed *ad collectam*, meaning at the place of gathering. Then when the pope (or priest) arrived at the church for Mass he would then pray another "collect" or opening prayer. When this custom of praying two "collect" prayers and processing to church for Mass died out, then the opening prayer was called a collect, and we were encouraged to "collect" our intentions for the Mass.

You will notice that the collect prayer is short: address to God and petition of God. Sometimes it refers to the feast or season being celebrated. At other times it is a very general acknowledgment of our need for God's mercy. On weekdays that are not special feasts or seasons, the priest may choose the opening prayer from a number of options in the *Sacramentary* under the heading of "Votive Masses and Masses and Prayers for Various Needs and Occasions." Or he may use any of the prayers assigned for the Sundays of Ordinary Time. Careful selection of these options can enhance daily celebrations and prevent them from becoming routine by the proclamation of the same prayers.

V.

LITURGY OF THE WORD

31. Who decides the cycle of readings in the *Lectionary* and why?

Your question is straightforward and direct but not that easy to answer. The simple answer would be the Vatican under the auspices of the Sacred Congregation for Divine Worship. But that is still rather vague. You see, the reforms of the liturgy after Vatican II were anonymous in the sense that they were officially endorsed by the popes at the time (and therefore had the highest authority of the church behind them), but we do not always know exactly who did what behind the scenes. Let me try to explain.

The Liturgy Constitution of Vatican II was the clarion call for the reform of all the rites of the Roman liturgy. It also contained the first official directives indicating the scope of the reforms to be undertaken. As for the reform of the readings at Mass, the Liturgy Constitution states that "the treasures of the Bible are to be opened up more lavishly, so that a richer share in God's word may be provided for the faithful. In this way a more representative portion of holy Scripture will be read to the people in the course of a prescribed number of years" (n. 51). As with the reform of all the other parts of the liturgy, the task of revising the readings for Mass was entrusted to a study group of the Vatican agency responsible for the reform (called the Consilium). According to the secretary for that body, Archbishop Annibale Bugnini, this was "one of the most difficult tasks of the entire reform: the reorganization of the readings for Mass." Because Archbishop Bugnini had firsthand knowledge of the process of the reform (and wrote about it) we know that the two chief architects of this work were Gaston Fontaine (Canada) and Cipriano Vagaggini (Italy). Vagaggini was very involved at every step of the process of preparing the Liturgy Constitution and the reform of many parts of the liturgy, while Fontaine surrendered his post in Canada in 1964 to be at the disposal of the Consilium largely to work on the *Lectionary*.

The basis of the lectionary study group's work was a study of the arrangement of readings that have been used for Mass from the patristic times through the Middle Ages and, of course, the previous Tridentine structure of readings. Some of these sources were lists of texts; other sources were actual books of readings. These books were lectionaries and gospel books. Perhaps you recall that in the Tridentine rite we used a missal which contained all the prayers and readings for Mass. In the earlier centuries of the church's life, however, the *Lectionary* was a separate book containing the scripture readings. Similarly the *Sacramentary* was the book containing the prayers of the Mass said by the priest, the *Antiphonal* was the book containing the chants sung by the schola/choir/congregation. All these were compressed into one book, the missal, when the priest's role dominated and he did all the parts of the Mass himself. With the restoration of the variety of roles in the liturgy, the decision was made to return to the former practice of having several books for the celebration of Mass. The *Lectionary*, therefore, contains the readings only. The study group assigned with the task of reforming the list of scripture readings, therefore, made several decisions about the shape of the *Lectionary* as a liturgical book. Very often the readings were chosen to reflect the feast being celebrated, for example, the resurrection gospels for Easter or the accounts of Christ's birth for Midnight Mass at Christmas. The answer to the next question can help fill out details about the present shape of our *Lectionary*.

32. Can you help me understand the structure of the *Lectionary*—both for Sundays and weekdays?

Generally speaking we can say that there are two sets of readings for weekday Masses and three sets for Sundays in what we call the season of the year or Ordinary Time. For the seasons of Advent, Christmas, Lent and Easter there are three sets of readings for Sundays but one set for the weekdays. My term "sets of readings" is more often than not referred to in the literature on the present liturgy as a cycle of readings, but whatever term is used, the point is the same: namely, that for every Sunday in Ordinary Time in the liturgical year readings are assigned according to a plan whereby one set of readings on a given Sunday is proclaimed once every three years and that on each Sunday three scripture readings are assigned—Old Testament, New Testament and gospel. The plan for the three sets of readings is such that each of the synoptic gospels (Matthew, Mark and Luke) can be proclaimed in a given calendar year. Hence the reference you sometimes see to the first cycle (Year A) called the year of Matthew, the second cycle (Year B) as the year of Mark, and the third cycle (Year C) as the year of Luke. Over the more than thirty weeks that make up Ordinary Time, each of these gospels is proclaimed in order, which is called the continuous reading of the gospel (the Latin term is *lectio continua*). The first reading for all these Sundays is from the Old Testament, and the particular text chosen for a particular Sunday is determined by the fact that it is judged to have an echo or is a prelude to what the gospel proclaims. What follows, the responsorial psalm, is meant to be a prayerful reiteration of that first reading (and should be sung, because the psalms are songs). That means that there is a thematic unity among the gospels, Old Testament readings and psalms for Ordinary Time Sundays. The second reading is taken from the epistles of St. Paul, and sections of these letters are proclaimed in order (like the gospels, a *lectio continua*). Therefore, on each Sunday in Ordinary Time you have two major themes from the readings that can be the bases for the homily that day.

On the weekdays of Ordinary Time you have a similar continuous reading of the gospels each day, but for weekdays we hear all the synoptic gospels read in order over the course of the year. The *Lectionary* gives us the gospel of Mark from the first week of Ordinary Time through the ninth week, the gospel of Matthew from the tenth week through the twenty-first week and the gospel of Luke from the twenty-second week through the thirty-third week. Now when the cycle comes to the first reading on weekdays of Ordinary Time, the texts selected are chosen to allow a continuous reading of a book of the Bible other than the gospels, again in order. But like the arrangement for Sundays, the psalm is chosen to be a prayerful reiteration of that first reading. The reason I said that there were two sets of weekday readings is because there are two sets of first readings for weekdays, proclaimed on alternate years, while the gospel is the same every year. (These first readings are referred to as Year I and Year II.)

When it comes to the special seasons of Advent, Christmas, Lent and Easter, the familiar pattern of three readings on Sundays remains. The choice of precisely which readings and why depends on a number of factors, and all of it is explained in the Introduction to the *Lectionary for Mass*. Let me give one example. In the season of Lent on the first Sunday in all three years of the *Lectionary*, all the gospels are about Jesus' temptation (again from the synoptics) and on the second Sunday the gospels recount his transfiguration (from the synoptics). What happens for the next three weeks in the A cycle, however, is a shift to the gospel of John: chapters 4, 9 and 11. These three texts proclaim the dialogue of Jesus with the Samaritan woman (Jn 4), the cure of the man born blind (Jn 9) and the raising of the dead man Lazarus (Jn 11). The reason why these gospels are specially chosen is *both* traditional and theological *at the same time*. From the fourth century on these texts were chosen to be proclaimed during Lent to remind those already baptized and to let those to be baptized at Easter know what baptism means—new life in Christ. Hence, the symbol of water (the Samaritan woman at the well), the symbol of light (blind man now able to see) and the notion of real life through faith in Jesus (the dead man Lazarus raised up), which are proclaimed on these Sundays, are the very symbols used in baptism at the Easter vigil, when the elect are baptized and candidates make their faith profession in the Catholic Church.

This notion of history and theology is also operative in the way much of the *Lectionary* for these same seasons has come about. For example, the scripture readings during the weekdays of Lent are the same each year, which texts stress themes related to baptism, reconciliation and identification with the paschal dying and rising of Christ. In the season of Easter, as you probably have noticed, we never read the Old Testament, and the gospels are always from John. Why? Liturgical tradition insists that in Christ we are a new creation, and that the old covenant cedes in emphasis to the new covenant in Christ in a special way during this season. Hence, the first reading is from the Acts of the Apostles to show how the risen Christ worked in the early church and continues to work among us now. The gospel of John was chosen because, from the time of St. Irenaeus on, it was regarded as "the spiritual gospel," much less concerned with details of Jesus' earthly life than with how we are identified with Christ and abide in God through him. We proclaim it for the fifty days of Easter to deepen our experience of our life in the risen Christ.

I hope all this doesn't sound too confusing! Simply put, please understand that there is a rhyme and reason to the *Lectionary*. What's the best way to understand it? I'd recommend your reading the Introduction to the *Lectionary* to understand the rationale for the texts selected and to gain insight into the theological meaning of the proclamation of the scriptures at Mass. Second, I'd recommend your reviewing and praying over the scripture readings for the following Sunday (and weekdays too) in order to get a sense of their breadth and implications for your life here and now. I'd say it is impossible to really experience the fullness of the readings at Mass without this preparation. After a while I'm sure the mechanics of what I have tried to explain will become both clear and less important and the experience of applying the scriptures to your life and living more completely in God will happen.

33. Is it true that Protestant churches proclaim the same readings we do on Sundays? What does this mean ecumenically?

At the same time that Pope Paul VI endorsed and officially sanctioned the use of *The Roman Missal* revised after Vatican II (1969) he officially endorsed the *Lectionary for Mass*, which contains perhaps the most far reaching organization of biblical readings for Mass that the Catholic Church has ever had. A very significant outgrowth of the adoption of this lectionary for our church has been its adoption (more or less) by a number of other Christian churches. So on a recent Sunday morning that at the eucharistic liturgies celebrated by members of neighboring Catholic, Episcopal, Lutheran, Presbyterian and Disciples of Christ Churches, all listened to the same passages from the scriptures. Therefore, you are quite right to point out the ecumenical implications of this phenomenon, one not directly planned, but a very significant outgrowth of the Second Vatican Council. How did this "quiet ecumenism" come about?

In 1978 the (North American) Consultation on Common Texts set to work on determining a more or less common set of scripture readings for Sundays that Christian churches could adopt. The resulting *Common Lectionary* was published in 1982 and a decade later a revised set of readings was published as *The Revised Common Lectionary*. These lectionaries are based on the Roman Catholic *Lectionary* and the discussions that led to the publication of these lectionaries had Roman Catholics as participants in the process.

An underlying principle of liturgical study (which I have repeatedly used in this book) is *lex orandi, lex credendi*—what we pray shapes what we believe. Now this is true not just for the prayers of the Mass but also for the scriptures we proclaim. As the Catholic Church still strives to reemphasize the value of biblical proclamation at Mass (and at all liturgies), the fact that we have such similar lectionary structures can only help to enhance our spiritual and theological ties across the lines of our various denominations. If it is true that "the family that prays together, stays together," who knows what ecumenical ties will be fostered by churches that pray over the same biblical readings week after week?

34. Which readings are required and which are optional? For example, my wife and I chose readings for our wedding, but the Sunday scriptures seemed to be required.

One of the most important features of the present lectionary structure for Mass is that it provides scripture readings for every day of the year, and unless there are important exceptions (which I'll soon describe), the readings are required and are not optional (see Introduction to the *Lectionary for Mass,* nn. 318–20). Sometimes during the week a special feast day occurs with scripture readings that are specially chosen for that day (e.g., Ascension, St. John the Baptist and so forth). On these days the special readings take the place of those in the weekday *Lectionary.* When this occurs, the priest should look ahead to the whole week's readings to determine whether the daily readings omitted for that special feast day should be combined and proclaimed together with the weekday readings the day before or after the feast (see *Lectionary* Introduction, n. 319).

Perhaps an illustration is the best way to make my point. As I mentioned in my answer to question 32, each of the synoptic gospels is proclaimed on the weekdays in Ordinary Time. Let's say that while we are proclaiming the gospel of Matthew in the weekday *Lectionary* that readings assigned for a special feast were to supersede the proclamation of the Beatitudes (Mt 5) assigned to that weekday. Now because of the importance of the Beatitudes for understanding the whole of the gospel of Matthew, the priest would be well advised to add this gospel to the gospel to be proclaimed on the day before or after the feast (which day contains its own readings). This way the community can have the benefit of hearing the integrity of chapter 5 of Matthew as the gospel reading that week.

However, there are occasions, like your wedding, which are called ritual Masses, when other scripture texts can be chosen that would replace the weekday readings. In this case you would have the opportunity to choose from a lectionary that has been prepared for weddings (just as there are lectionaries for baptisms, ordinations and so forth) in order that the scriptures proclaimed for that ritual Mass would reflect the specific sacrament being celebrated. But even here, on the Sundays of the special seasons of Advent, Christmas, Lent and Easter the scripture readings cannot be changed. The reason? The scripture readings for those seasons are specially selected and are regarded as extremely important for the whole church's celebration of the fullness of Christmas and Easter.

35. In what way should the psalm be considered responsorial, and is it supposed to be sung?

Allow me to cite two famous church fathers from the patristic era and a contemporary church document to answer your question. The notion that the psalm after the first reading is responsorial and that the congregation should respond to the cantor is found in the liturgical writings of St. Augustine in the early fifth century. But by the end of the sixth century it had become a virtuoso piece to be sung by the deacon only! Therefore, in 595 St. Gregory the Great forbade this solo singing. As choirs and scholas took over most of the people's sung participation in the Mass, this psalm was reduced to a couple of verses (called the "gradual") and was regularly combined with the alleluia before the gospel. The Introduction to the *Lectionary for Mass* cites this as an important, integral element of the Word of God (n.19) and that every means available should be used to facilitate the congregation's singing (n.21). This Introduction states that the psalm is led by the cantor or psalmist from the lectern, which location shows its importance as part of the Liturgy of the Word.

The *Lectionary for Mass* presumes that the psalm is sung and offers two options. Either it is sung by the cantor with the congregation repeating the sung refrain after each verse, or it can be sung straight through, either by the cantor alone or by the congregation together. The only exception to this preferred practice is found in the same Introduction (n.22) stating that "when not sung, the responsorial psalm is to be recited in a manner conducive to meditation on the Word of God."

Let me make a final comment on the psalm's importance. The restoration of the proclamation of the scriptures at Mass in the vernacular is for the spiritual benefit of the whole church. In a literal and figurative sense the Book of Psalms is the church's prayer book. It contains the range of human emotions and reflects the spiritual ups and downs that believers always experience. The psalms are both Israel's and the

Christian church's sung prayer. They were originally set to music and should be sung. As a part of the Liturgy of the Word, one advantage of the sung psalm is that it provides a change from the spoken proclamation of the readings and offers the congregation the opportunity to reflect about what had been proclaimed through song and personal prayer.

In theory the other sung parts of the Roman rite for Mass (entrance, offertory and communion) are taken from the psalms. In practice, however, to facilitate easier participation by the congregation, the American bishops allowed the use of other hymns and songs that the people know to substitute for the singing of psalms at these parts of the liturgy. However, the responsorial psalm is not to be replaced by any other song, and because it may be the only psalm that the congregation sings and hears, it has even greater importance than if it were one of four psalms sung at Mass.

The "bottom line" is to follow Augustine and Gregory, and you can't go wrong!

36. What is the gospel acclamation and is it required?

The purpose of the gospel acclamation is to set up, or to introduce, the proclamation of the gospel that follows it. It introduces what we believe to be the "good news" of the words and deeds of Christ. In all the seasons of the church year except for Lent (which does not use the alleluia from Ash Wednesday until the Easter vigil), this part of the Mass is commonly called the alleluia. Structurally, it normally consists of the alleluia first sung by the cantor or choir, repeated by everyone, a verse from scripture sung by the cantor or choir, and a final alleluia sung by all. The source of the scripture verse varies. On Sundays during the seasons of Advent, Christmas, Lent and Easter and on feast days (e.g., solemnities of the Lord, feasts of apostles and so forth) these verses are provided in the *Lectionary for Mass* and usually refer to the specific gospel proclamation that follows. In Ordinary Time the verse is chosen from a number provided as options in the Lectionary (n. 164 for the sixteen options for these Sundays). On weekdays these verses are chosen from the options provided in the *Lectionary* for the seasons or Ordinary Time (which choices are normally found collected at the end of the readings assigned for that season).

The Introduction to the *Lectionary* provides for a rather wide variety of options for Masses when there are only two readings: either the responsorial psalm and gospel acclamation together, or responsorial psalm only or gospel acclamation only. In any case, the use of a period of silence after the readings and after whatever is sung is pastorally valuable to allow the meaning of the scriptures to be pondered and accepted by all. Sometimes a congregation will regularly choose an option from the possible choices because of the particular nature or demands of the liturgical season. For example, because the alleluia is not used during Lent, a parish may choose to use the responsorial psalm on Lenten weekdays. Alternatively, because the alleluia is restored at the Easter vigil after not being sung during Lent, a parish might choose to emphasize the verse before the gospel rather than the psalm on weekdays of Easter. However, the "downside" of this option is that the psalms, which in my opinion get short shrift in pastoral practice in the reformed Mass, would wind up not being used for a period of fifty days.

Given these and the many other options in the structure of the present Mass, the keen pastoral caution of the General Instruction of the Roman Missal (n. 313) should always be recalled: "In planning the celebration, then, the priest should consider the general spiritual good of the assembly rather than his personal outlook. He should be mindful that the choice of texts is to be made in consultation with the ministers and others who have a function in the celebration, including the faithful in regard to the parts that more directly belong to them."

37. Do we have to have a children's Liturgy of the Word? Is it not correct to have a children's Mass? If not, why not?

I've already referred to the important document from 1973 called the *Directory for Masses with Children* as a major contribution to the liturgical formation that children can and should receive about the Mass and about their particular participation in the Mass. One of the principal advantages of this liturgical document is that it is not just a "how to" set of norms. Rather, it is like the other General Instructions to all the revised liturgical rites because it contains a generous section (chapter 1) on the liturgical, catechetical and pedagogical value of involving children in the liturgy. The document describes two common pastoral situations. One describes Masses with adults in which children participate (chapter 2). It is in this section that you will find a description of a Liturgy of the Word, including the homily, with the children in a separate room from the body of the church (n. 17). This statement has led many parishes to have a separate Liturgy of the Word for children at one or another Sunday Mass. However, the consistent principle in this *Directory* is that the children should be instructed in how to participate in the regular Mass and that they should be made to feel a part of the assembly. This can happen when the priest addresses them specifically in some comments (e.g., in the introduction to Mass, in some petitions to the intercessions and even in the homily) at Masses when the children are not separated from the adults for the Liturgy of the Word. In addition to this *Roman Directory,* the bishops of the United States have also published a *Lectionary for Masses with Children,* which at times simplifies some terms and shortens some scripture texts to suit children's comprehension. The children return to the main Sunday assembly at the presentation of the gifts and remain with their parents for the rest of the Mass.

The second pastoral situation that the *Directory* envisions is at Masses with children in which only a few adults participate. The document presumes that this circumstance occurs normally on weekdays (n. 20). The document reiterates the important principle that even when parts of the Mass are adapted to the children that "it is always necessary to keep in mind that these eucharistic celebrations must lead toward the celebration of Mass with adults" (n. 21). It is in this section of the document about these celebrations that we find the statement that "one of the adults may speak to the children after the gospel, especially if the priest finds it difficult to adapt himself to the mentality of the children" (n. 24).

In my experience the problem with a special Liturgy of the Word for children or with Masses specially planned and celebrated for them is not the theory; rather, it's what happens in practice. Sometimes, because of a lack of resources or even a lack of appreciating what a Liturgy of the Word is, what can happen is that children leave the congregation for what resembles instruction on the scriptures and an activity like coloring or some similar pursuit. What we need to recall is the importance that the *Directory* places on this special Liturgy of the Word as a liturgy, which means an event that involves the children in listening, singing, praying in silence and in offering petitions in the intercessions. Since the aim is to progressively engage them in the regular adult Mass, the more we can mirror the regular structure of the Sunday Mass at these special liturgies of the Word, the better.

38. Why do some people trace the cross on their heads, lips and hearts at the gospel?

I also see this a lot and can remember it from the former Tridentine Mass. But in point of fact, this ritual gesture is not found in the ritual description of the Mass. The present missal states that at the proclamation of the gospel the deacon (or priest if there is no deacon) sings or says "A reading from the holy gospel according to…," and then it states that "he makes the sign of the cross on the book, and then on his forehead, lips and breast." The meaning of at least part of this is taken from the blessing that the priest gives to the deacon (or that the priest says to himself if there is no deacon): "…may the Lord be in your heart and on your lips that you may worthily proclaim his gospel." This gesture is important as a nonverbal reminder to the one who proclaims the gospel that it is indeed "good news" and that in proclaiming this text the deacon or priest should revere its message in what he thinks (mind), in what he says (lips) and in his heart (breast). The fact that many in the congregation imitate this gesture may well signal their own willingness to do the same thing. Even though it is not prescribed for the congregation it is not something that I'd take away from them. After all, liturgy involves gestures and movement, and this addition to the congregation's participation seems quite logical and legitimate.

39. Our priest announced that Sunday's homily will be dramatized by the youth group at all Masses. We do the same for Christmas Eve. Is this correct? What's the difference between a sermon and a homily?

Let me take the second part of your question first. The term "homily" comes from the Greek word *homilia* and refers to speech that is more familiar and "true to life" than the language of high rhetoric often associated with classical oratory. It is a term that has been recovered with the reform of the liturgy to indicate the kind of public speech that follows the proclamation of the gospel. It is intended to explain "the biblical word of God proclaimed in the readings or some other texts of the liturgy [and] must always lead the community of the faithful to celebrate the Eucharist wholeheartedly" (*Lectionary*, Introduction, n. 24). It is recommended that it be well prepared, not too long or too short and suited to all those present, even children and the uneducated (n. 24). Now that's a tall order! And what a challenge for the presiding priest who (normally) is the one to deliver it.

Strictly speaking, therefore, the homily is not a sermon, since the subject matter for sermons is any kind of religious theme. Similarly, a dramatization at the homily would not seem to fit the criteria just cited. Let's take the example of Christmas Eve. Often, what happens is the dramatization of the Christmas story. This means that as the gospel is proclaimed, young people, usually, act out or dramatize what we are hearing. Or sometimes, after the gospel, a dramatization of the events of Christ's birth at Bethlehem occurs with a script that echoes the gospel. Or still again, this involves the people engaged in speaking and acting out their parts. Now the problem with such dramatizations is not the medium so much as it is the message. The purpose of the homily is to draw out the message of the good news for us here and now. The homily follows upon the gospel as its extension, its application. It is not meant to be a repetition or summary of what we have already heard. It is intended to help us penetrate and experience more fully what we have already heard and to lead us to celebrate the Eucharist that follows wholeheartedly. Dramatizations can be legitimate vehicles for catechesis or instruction about the gospels. But they do not serve the liturgy because they "freeze the frame" on what happened in history, whereas the purpose of the homily is to help us experience God's saving good news here and now.

From a pastoral viewpoint, what often lies behind the dramatization in the homily is that this affords a way for the youth to be more fully involved in the Mass. My recommendation in such a case is to involve the youth in a number of ways in the liturgy itself and in preparing for it. There is nothing that says that all liturgical roles are reserved for people over a certain age. Having young people involved in music ministry, in reading, offering petitions for the prayer of the faithful, serving at the altar and so forth can enhance their participation and experience of the liturgy. The only caution I would offer is that roles are meant to serve the liturgy and that those chosen to fulfill them should be able to. Hence, for example, those who read should have that ability. Anything childish or that would derogate from the beauty and flow of the liturgy should be avoided. With regard to participation, involving some young people in a group that helps the priest prepare the homily can help the final result to resonate more fully with the lived experience of the community. And that, after all, is one of the most important aspects of what homily preparation and execution is all about!

40. Recently our pastor removed the worship aids from the church. Now I can't read the readings before Mass. Why did Father take the worship aids away?

From what you've read so far I am sure it has become clear that one of the main goals of the reform of the Mass is to engage us in an action that uses and respects all our faculties: sight, sound, smell, taste and touch. One of the things that helped people to follow the former Mass and to "participate" by reading along with the priest was the publication of small missals in English (often called hand missals). With the common practice of using the vernacular for the Mass we have no need for the same kind of help for us to follow the Mass. Now we are able to hear the readings in our own language, to engage our bodies in more gestures than before and to sing at times when the choir formerly sang on our behalf. Theoretically at least, because of the restored ministry of reader, we no longer should read the scriptures at Mass. Rather, we should listen to the reader's and deacon's proclamation. The more we raise our heads to see and attune our ears to what we hear, the more the Mass becomes a communal event in which we actively participate and the less it remains something conducted in the sanctuary that we follow along with such things as a hand missal.

Why, then, you might ask, did we "invent" the worship aid? We did so precisely to enable people to become familiar with the revised Mass texts and to enable them to participate by providing the correct responses throughout the Mass and to aid them in singing the vernacular music, which was also printed in the worship aids. That the scriptures and the presidential prayers were printed in these worship aids recalled the hand missal custom, but in fact it was probably a large mistake to include them in the worship aid. Why? Because their inclusion along with the spoken and sung people's responses may well have signaled that people were to read along as they had done before rather than to engage themselves in new ways in the "new" Mass.

At the same time, I fully realize that some people have difficulty in hearing. Given the fact that people live longer and the aging often experience hearing loss, it is appropriate that some provision be made whereby they are able to follow the Mass and to participate in it. One way is to have several copies of the worship aid (perhaps in a "large print" edition) available for them at the church door. Another option would be to have a bound worship aid available for them that contains the readings and prayers of the day.

My final thought (as I have already said) is that we need to come to Mass prepared in mind and heart. This means that we have prayed over the scriptures that will be proclaimed on a given day. This makes the Liturgy of the Word easier to follow for all of us. It also allows our attention to be focused on how the homily takes what has been proclaimed and applies it to our daily lives. Some parishes cite the following week's readings in their weekly bulletins precisely to allow for this preparation. The fact that the worship aids may have been taken away does not mean that we ought not be concerned about how we prepare for Sunday Mass.

41. Is there really a difference between when the scriptures are read in the liturgy and when I pray over them at home?

Your question is very focused and reflects a deepening appreciation for the proclamation of the word as an essential part of the way we experience Christ's salvation in the Mass. But to answer it let me use an example from the Book of Genesis to affirm that there is a difference. In the first chapter of Genesis we read of the way God created the heavens and the earth during the seven days of creation—it was through God's speaking that things came to be. Consider, for example, the first day when God created light: "…then God said 'Let there be light,' and there was light…" (vs. 3). It's as simple and yet as profound as that. God speaks and things happen. The Liturgy of the Word is essentially an action of divine address and our response to it. The scriptures are proclaimed and in the act of being proclaimed they reveal God's divine plans and irrevocable covenant. In the act of proclamation, that covenant is made operative for us here and now. Another example is from the beginning of Jesus' public ministry in Luke's gospel. In chapter 4 Jesus returns to Nazareth, enters the synagogue, proclaims the text from Isaiah about the suffering servant (Is 61:1f.) and then declares, "…today this Scripture passage is fulfilled in your hearing" (Lk 4:21). Whenever we proclaim the scriptures, what is described is fulfilled in our hearing. What the text proclaims about the words and deeds of Jesus happens to and for us now. In other words, what happens when the scriptures are proclaimed is an event of salvation, not just a description of salvation. The proclaimed scriptures are our present experience of covenant relatedness to God through Christ, not just a description of what the covenant is like.

The very structure of the Liturgy of the Word reveals the fact that we view it as an event of our salvation. In the liturgy we engage in a dialogue. God speaks through the scriptures and we accept and commit ourselves to them by saying "Thanks be to God" or "Praise to you Lord Jesus Christ." The divine address to us through the word invites our human response of acceptance and commitment. We do this through the acclamations at the end of the proclaimed texts, the responsorial psalm and the gospel acclamation. One of the purposes of the homily is to draw out some aspect of the proclamation of the scriptures and apply this good news to our needs and lives here and now.

Take the example of the parable of the prodigal son from Luke 15. This text is now used in our present *Lectionary for Mass* as well as in the Liturgy of the Word for communal penance services. Every time we hear this parable proclaimed in the liturgy, God's act of acceptance, forgiveness and reconciliation happens. What the father does for his son in the parable is what God does for us in Christ through our hearing of this parable. The kingdom of God—God's designs and actions on our behalf—is incarnate through the Word proclaimed and ratified in the eucharistic meal we share. The way we communicate as humans—through both words and gestures—is the way we experience God's salvation in the Mass.

Two comments about the rite for the proclamation of the gospel may help illustrate this. At the end of the gospel the deacon or priest kisses the gospel book. When he does so he says to himself, "By the words of the gospel may our sins be blotted out." This is a brief reminder of what it means that the gospel is proclaimed—we experience salvation again and again. Another example is from the Latin introduction to the (former) *Lectionary.* Each gospel passage was introduced by the Latin phrase *in illo tempore*, commonly translated as "at that time." Now that looks like a reference to when Jesus originally said or did what the gospel describes. In fact it's the opposite. To declare "at that time" means that what Jesus did once in saving history he does here and now for us. This little phrase was a constant reminder that the gospels are not descriptions of historical reminiscences. Rather, they are one of the privileged ways that we continue to live in God's covenant love.

Now with all of this said you may be thinking that I am neglecting or ignoring the value of praying over the scriptures. Not at all. In fact, one of the most important revolutions that has taken place in our church since Vatican II has been the way people have taken to reading and praying over the scriptures, individually and in groups. The ancient term for this is *lectio divina*, meaning a holy reading of the Bible. This kind of personal prayer is essential for us to experience the Liturgy of the Word for what it truly is. We need to know the stories of the scriptures through personal prayer in order to take them to heart as fully as possible through the Liturgy of the Word. Personal reflection on the scriptures gives us the foundation to appreciate even more fully what happens when the scriptures are proclaimed at Mass.

42. Is the creed always necessary at Mass?

The present Roman rite prescribes the profession of faith at Masses on Sundays and solemnities. The text of the creed is a combination of the faith professions from the Councils of Nicea (325) and Constantinople (381). More commonly, it is referred to as the "Nicene Creed." At Masses with children the (simpler) Apostles' Creed may be said. The liturgical background here is from the profession of faith in Father, Son and Spirit that formed the baptismal question-and-answer dialogue with those to be baptized. The inclusion of the full text of the creed started in parts of Europe as a reaction to heresies about the divinity of Christ as early as the fifth century. It was incorporated into the Roman Mass in the eleventh century.

In the present Roman Mass the creed is not used at the Easter vigil because the community professes its faith through the baptismal question-and-answer form used by those being initiated and received into the church that night. On Easter Sunday itself the Nicene Creed is usually replaced by the same dialogue question-and-answer form of the profession of faith from the Easter vigil Mass.

43. Are the general intercessions the same as the prayer of the faithful? Who writes these?

The simple answer to the first part of your question is yes. But a little historical background might help. The phrase "prayer of the faithful" was used to distinguish these prayers as being said by the already baptized as opposed to the catechumens, who were not yet among "the faithful" and hence were not present for these prayers. The more common term today is "general intercessions," which signifies that these are prayers for the whole church and for the church as it intercedes for the whole world.

The structure of the prayer that we commonly use at Mass contains an introduction by the priest (a variation on "let us pray," not itself a prayer to God), the statement of petitions and the congregation's response, and a concluding prayer by the priest. Classically, it was the deacon who announced the intentions because it was he who knew the particular needs of the community (who needed food, charity, who was sick, who had died and so forth). By exercising this liturgical role he reflected his ministry outside the Mass and thereby exemplified the unity of worship and Christian living.

As for who writes the general intercessions, there can be a number of answers. The Introduction to the *Lectionary* states that "the deacon, another minister, or some of the faithful may propose intentions that are short and phrased with a measure of flexibility" (n. 30). What is envisioned here is the involvement of the assembly in articulating petitions, whether spoken or written down. Some parishes enlist the aid of some laypeople in preparing the petitions in liturgy planning meetings; others have a box for people to drop them off as they enter church on Sunday, and some assign the task of composing them to a committee. Sometimes, however, for the sake of convenience, the prayer of the faithful is written by the priest and/or deacon. Certainly the letter of the recommendations in the *Lectionary* introduction and the spirit of the prayer as the "prayer of the faithful" would seem to invite participation "of the faithful" in preparing these prayers.

The appendix to the *Sacramentary* includes several sets of sample intercessions that coincide with the liturgical seasons. These are very helpful models for the general intercessions. Normally these prayers concern the needs of the church, the nation or world, those suffering for any particular reason, the sick and, finally, the deceased. Generally speaking the more universal and general this prayer is, the better, hence the prayers for the nation, world and so forth. But the more specific it is in naming the sick and the deceased of a particular community, the better, because it reflects certain communities that gather for the liturgy. But even here, the style of prayer is inclusive of individuals and all who are sick and all who have died.

The concluding prayer is done by the priest. Since the content of the prayer is not specified, the same creativity in composing the petitions would also be encouraged here.

44. Why are the people preparing to become Catholics sent away after the homily? Why can't they stay for the entire Mass?

What you are referring to is an ancient custom that has been revived in the present rites of the catechumenate (the period of up to three years for adults preparing for Christian initiation). From as early as the third century, and certainly strongly attested in the fourth and fifth centuries (in the writings of Saints Augustine, Cyril of Jerusalem, John Chrysostom), catechumens were "dismissed" from the Sunday Eucharist after the homily. Most often, there were prayers for the catechumens and a formula to "dismiss" them. It was only after the catechumens were dismissed that those who remained (the faithful) joined in the "prayer of the faithful." Catechumens were dismissed because they were not yet initiated into the church and therefore would not comprehend what was going on at the Eucharist, which action presumed that all would receive communion (which of course they could not). Sometimes called the *disciplina arcani,* "the discipline of the secret," this practice also reflected the fact that those not initiated would not know the doctrine or the theological meaning of what was occurring in the rest of the Mass. It was only after this period of the catechumenate that they would know about their faith to the extent that they could participate and know what they were doing at the liturgy. It was at the Easter vigil that they would share in the rites of the full Eucharist for the first time. That's why for the week after Easter the newly initiated would return to the bishop and learn all about the sacraments they had received at the vigil. We call these instructions the mystagogic catecheses, literally the "instructions on the sacred mysteries."

These historical precedents—and perhaps more importantly the theology behind them—caused the committee that revised the rites of adult initiation to include the dismissals as a regular feature of the Sunday Mass. Here, liturgical tradition grounds our present practice. But this is not to be understood as imitating an historical precedent for its own sake. What I am saying is that if we now do this only because we did it "once upon a time" and "older is better," then we risk delusion and we can appear to avoid the demands of the present. Clearly the secrecy factor about the Mass is now absent, given the fact that people can watch the Mass on television regularly, or on such special occasions as the liturgy of a papal funeral. So we can't be anachronistic and think that people do not know what is going on at Mass—especially if catechumens have already been coming to Mass for years! But what can become clear is that these dismissals can offer the catechumens (i.e., those not baptized) and the candidates for admission into the church (i.e., those already baptized in another Christian church) a time to be apart and to reflect more deeply on the Sunday scriptures under the direction of a catechist or teacher. In addition, the very fact of dismissing catechumens and candidates from the Sunday assembly can be a way to reinforce for those who remain who they are as baptized and confirmed members of the church, whose privilege it is to share in the Eucharist.

Bottom line: the dismissals are not meant to be penance or a diminishment of who the catechumens and candidates are; they are opportunities for all of us to look forward to their sacramental initiation at Easter and, in the meantime, to deepen our appreciation of what the Mass truly is.

VI.

LITURGY OF THE EUCHARIST

45. Why do we collect actual gifts for the poor at Mass only on Thanksgiving?

I suppose the simple answer to your question is *custom*, but a custom of a relatively recent vintage. It has really only been since Vatican II that Thanksgiving Day has "caught on" as a day to celebrate the Eucharist. In fact, in recent years I've heard priests say that this should be a holy day of obligation because it does what holy days originally did in Europe: gather the people for Mass on a holiday. Also, I suspect that many parishes experience a high level of active participation at Thanksgiving Day Mass because the assembly is an intentional community—people who want to be there and who often share in many of the parish ministries. Therefore, it is not surprising that on this day of special thanks we would remember the poor and the hungry by collecting actual gifts for them.

Actually this was among the earliest liturgical traditions of the church—to collect food for the needy as they presented the food to be used for the Eucharist. This custom died out and its place was taken by collecting monetary gifts. But again, the origin of this custom was to share our bounty with those in need. The General Instruction of the Roman Missal reflects some of these practices when it states that the "preparation of the gifts" is "the time to receive money or other gifts for the church or the poor brought by the faithful or collected at the Mass" (n.49). What is clearly underscored here is the association of eucharistic gifts with serving the poor and needy. Some parishes implement what is envisioned by collecting gifts in the church vestibule on a regular basis, indicating the community's care for the less fortunate.

In addition, the directives for the Evening Mass of the Lord's Supper on Holy Thursday state that "at the beginning of the Liturgy of the Eucharist, there may be a procession of the faithful with gifts for the poor." This is a significant statement because on this most solemn night when we commemorate the institution of the Eucharist, the church asks that we unite our liturgical service with service of the poor. Hence, whether it is on Thanksgiving, Holy Thursday, a Sunday Eucharist or at other times in connection with gathering for the Eucharist, the link between sharing eucharistic gifts and food for the poor is part of our tradition. This association should be upheld as a key value and a concrete expression of what the Mass signifies.

46. Where does the collection money go and how much should I put into the collection at Mass?

In answering the previous question I cited the directives of the *Missal,* which indicate that the money is collected for the church and the poor. This suggests that the financial contributions you make go for parish expenses (e.g., staff salaries, education expenses, plant maintenance and so forth) and whatever is designated for social justice concerns. With regard to how much you should contribute, I can offer the biblical admonition about tithing and a broader notion of what you might give to the community. In biblical terms (see Dt 14:22) the notion of tithing means that people were expected to give 10 percent of what they earned from their land. A rather strict interpretation of this injunction still applies today in some Christian churches, especially among the Baptists, as opposed to the custom whereby Catholics customarily give lesser sums. Part of the reason is that when civil governments oversaw the support of the Catholic faith in parts of Europe, this meant that the faithful were relied upon less and less for church support. Therefore, their giving habits adjusted accordingly.

In recent years the Catholic Church in America has sought to frame the discussion of what we give to the church community in terms of stewardship. This means that what we have been given is ours only in the sense that we are free to choose what to do with it for the common good. Part of stewardship is obviously money. But part of what we have been given for the common good concerns our God-given gifts and talents, which are also to be shared with others. The sound bite "time, talent, treasure" expresses the insight that what we have been given should be shared freely and joyfully with others. One way that some parishes help people explore the ways they can offer their talents is to publicize a range of tasks that can be done by any number of people—education, administration, home visiting, legislative advocacy, liturgical ministry, and so on. In this way the limited focus of "how much" in terms of dollars shifts to appreciating that what is *mine* really belongs to *us,* and that as a member of the church I am to share what I am and have with others. But now getting back to your original question—how much? A priest friend of mine advises his parishioners to start with what they receive as an hour's wage. That's the starting point for evaluating what they might consider giving as they work toward the biblical injunction of 10 percent of what I "have" for the Lord.

47. What kinds of things should be included in the offertory procession? We used to bring up the hosts and water and wine. Now we sometimes don't bring up the water. Why?

According to the General Instruction of the Roman Missal, the gifts that "the faithful [are] to present [are] the bread and wine" and "money or other gifts for the church or the poor brought by the faithful" (n. 49). Notice that it states precisely that the eucharistic gifts are "bread and wine" and not water. The rationale here is that these foods are the result of human planting, harvesting, productivity and manufacture. These are central to our act of self-giving because even though we usually do not bake the eucharistic bread or produce the eucharistic wine, as once was customary and expected, nevertheless these gifts reflect the end result of human manufacture and labor—labor brought to the liturgy as a sign of our dedication and willingness to give of our talents for the sake of others.

Behind this act of presenting the bread and wine for the Mass is the liturgical principle that what we consume at communion should be consecrated at the Mass being celebrated and that only if necessary should we use hosts from the tabernacle for distribution. The historical background here is that while this was the norm and custom through the Middle Ages, when the laity came to receive communion less and less, the emphasis for the Mass to be valid was placed on the priest's receiving communion from the bread and wine consecrated at that Mass. This was ratified and solidified by the liturgy and teaching of the Council of Trent. However, as early as the middle of the eighteenth century, the popes, beginning with Benedict XIV, began insisting that all the communion to be received was consecrated at each Mass. The reason was not just a liturgical nicety. He was concerned that if this did not occur, the sacrifice of the Mass would be seen as separated from the communion at Mass, and our theology taught that these were inseparable. Sacrifice and sacrament were one act that together were essential parts of the Mass. It was Pope Pius XII who reiterated this in modern times. The General Instruction of the Roman Missal summarizes this teaching and practice when it says:

"It is most desirable that the faithful receive the Lord's body from hosts consecrated at the same Mass and that, in instances when it is permitted, they share in the chalice. Then even through the signs communion will stand out more clearly as a sharing in the sacrifice actually being offered" (n.56 h).

48. Is the term "offertory" still proper to use today? I seem to recall in the former Mass that the offertory took much longer and had many more prayers and gestures. What happened?

Your question is very well phrased because you use what was a proper term according to the theology and the Mass of Trent. But it isn't any longer. Let me try to explain.

Much of the controversies regarding the Mass at the time of the Reformation focused on the concept of sacrifice. Debates raged over whether or not the Mass was a sacrifice, how it could be so, and whether the sacrifice of the Mass repeated or added anything to Christ's sacrifice on Calvary. In light of these disputes, the bishops at the Council of Trent were very clear to state that the Mass was a sacrifice. A common phrase that was used after Trent to describe the link between Calvary and the Mass was that the Mass was the "unbloody sacrifice of Calvary." Because the Catholic Church found itself so concerned about emphasizing the sacrificial nature of the Mass after the Council of Trent, it taught that the three principal parts of the Mass were the offertory, the consecration and the communion. When these terms were specified, they were interpreted to mean that we offered bread and wine at the offertory, that at the consecration they were changed into the body and blood of Christ and that after the priest received communion the sacrament and sacrifice of the Mass were made valid because these three actions had taken place. That's why the common understanding in the former rite of the Mass was that you committed no mortal sin if you arrived at Mass in time for the offertory.

In the revised *Missal* you no longer read about the offertory at this part of the Mass. In the General Instruction of the Roman Missal it's called the preparation of the gifts. In the actual text (of the ordinary of the Mass) in the *Missal* this rite is called the preparation of the altar and the gifts. This change in terminology signals a change in understanding that the purpose of this rite is to lead to the eucharistic prayer, not to diminish its prominence in any way. Whatever rites are associated with presenting bread and wine should be understood as preparatory for the transformation of the gifts that takes place in the consecration during the eucharistic prayer. You are quite right that in the former Mass the offertory was longer and had more ceremony. In fact, the priest raised up the host and the chalice at this point the way he did during the eucharistic prayer. He also said five prayers that echoed much of the theology of the Roman canon. The present rite is much more simplified and focuses on placing the gifts on the altar table.

The General Instruction states that "in the preparation of the gifts, the bread and wine are brought to the altar" (n.48, 1). What is interesting is that it also states that "it is desirable for the faithful to present the bread and wine which are accepted by the priest or deacon" (n.49). Hence, emphasis is placed on both people and priest at this part of the Mass and the rite is viewed as a simple transition to the proclamation of the eucharistic prayer.

Now, you may ask, is the term "offertory" or "offering" obsolete? Not really. In fact, what has occurred in the present revision of the Mass is that the verb form "we offer" is found in some form or other in every eucharistic prayer. In the Roman canon, used from the early church through today, it states, "We offer to you, God of glory and majesty, this holy and perfect sacrifice." This phrase refers to the consecrated bread and wine, now become the one perfect sacrifice, the very paschal mystery of Christ himself. When we say "we offer" these gifts we signify that it is the once offered and unique sacrifice of Christ that we offer to the Father through Christ himself in the unity of the Holy Spirit. The more traditional place for the prayer of offering is here at the very section of the canon (and the other eucharistic prayers) where we commemorate Christ's dying, rising, ascension and eternal intercession on our behalf at the right hand of God the Father.

In sum: we *present* gifts as we prepare the altar; we *offer* them as the sacrifice of Christ himself to the Father in the eucharistic prayer.

49. Should the altar really be called the table?

In the church's post–Vatican II liturgical writings it is called both the altar and the table. In the General Instruction of the Roman Missal it states clearly that "at the altar (Latin: *altare*) the sacrifice of the cross is made present under sacramental signs. It is also the table of the Lord *(est etiam mensa Domini),* and the people of God are called together to share in it" (n. 259). What we have here is a good example of a useful juxtaposition of two emphases whereby the same Eucharist is understood to be both a sacrifice and a holy meal to be shared. In the revised liturgical documents, when the sacrificial nature of the Mass is emphasized, the term "altar" is used, and when the communal banquet is emphasized, the term "table" is used. Most often these emphases and terms are found together in post–Vatican II literature so that sacrifice and banquet as well as altar and table should be understood as inclusive of each other, and not separated.

In the Rite of the Dedication of a Church and an Altar (1977), this same description from the General Instruction of the Roman Missal is repeated. But the rite also adds the important sentence: "...by instituting in the form of a sacrificial meal the memorial of the sacrifice he was about to offer the Father on the altar of the cross, Christ made holy the table where the community would come to celebrate their Passover" (n. 3). In the following paragraph the rite states "...the Christian altar is by its very nature properly the table of sacrifice and of the paschal banquet. It is:

—a unique altar on which the sacrifice of the cross is perpetuated in mystery throughout the ages until Christ comes;

—a table at which the Church's children come together to give thanks to God and receive the body and blood of Christ" (n. 4).

In Christian antiquity it was common to say that "the altar is Christ." Therefore, it is quite proper that we bow to it as a sign of reverence at the beginning and at the end of Mass.

Part of the difficulty I see today when people discuss the reform of the Mass, especially when they complain about its not being the same as it was before the reform, is that the rhetoric that is used is often polarizing. It often separates what should not be separated. When some people insist on the sacrificial aspect of the Mass, they are correct in insisting that this emphasis not be lost. But at the same time they should be equally prepared to accept the reemphasis that current church teaching places on the Eucharist as a sacrificial meal. The same is true for some discussions today about the terminology for "altar" and "table." The more we can use both terms the more faithful we are to church tradition—to all of it, not just that from Trent on—and to the contemporary liturgical directives of the church.

Very little is said about the size or shape of the altar in either the General Instruction of the Roman Missal or the rite for its dedication. These texts specify that it should be fixed, freestanding so that the priest can walk around it and that the biblical symbolism of its being made of stone should be preserved. The conference of bishops, however, has indicated that it can be made of "any becoming, solid, and finely wrought material" (Rite of Dedication, n. 9). Most usually the altar is a slight rectangle or a somewhat squared block of solid material. However, there is nothing in church legislation that forbids it from being oblong or rounded. One of my friends, a Maryknoll missioner stationed in Hong Kong, was responsible for constructing a new church and parish center in the suburbs of the center of the city. Because the Chinese customarily eat at round tables, he designed the altar in an oblong shape precisely to underscore the fact that the Mass is a communal meal. I also suspect that part of his motivation was to capitalize on the emphasis that the Chinese culture places on the act of dining together. The cultural practice of dining together can be an effective metaphor helpful for explaining not only the nature of the Mass but for understanding the very essence of Christianity—as a religion of communal faith and shared identity. This in itself could be quite a countercultural reality in the face of the kind of individualism that marks much of the theology and practice of Eastern religions. Becoming a convert to Christianity in general, and to the sacramental system of Catholicism in particular, requires quite a shift in outlook regarding the underlying purpose of religion. Obviously for my priest friend, the symbolic custom of familial dining at a round table for daily food serves as a significant symbolic link to interpret the theology of the Mass as well as the nature and theology of the Christian church.

50. Why does the church throughout the whole world have to use bread and wine for Mass?

The short answer to your question is that we do what Jesus did. The more appropriate answer has three parts: Why did Jesus do what he did; what do bread and wine signify; and what does custom have to do with this?

Why did Jesus use bread and wine? The scriptures repeatedly tell us that he was an observant Jew. In his role as a rabbi and teacher, he would follow Jewish custom and host his disciples at a weekly sabbath meal. In the case of the Last Supper, he was host at a meal with strong Passover overtones. The memorial meal of the Jews commemorated their liberation from bondage in Egypt. They told the story of their freedom and shared in the banquet commemorating it, a meal that included bread and wine. Now these foods are the staples of the Middle Eastern diet to this day. These foods were the means Jesus used to commemorate his coming passing over from death to new life. His act of blessing bread and wine at the Last Supper involved a solemn declaration that from now on it was his passover they would commemorate and their/our unity through and with him to new life. The command "do this in memory of me" is the basis for our engaging in this same kind of blessing prayer at Mass—words spoken over bread and wine. The bread and wine of Judaism's sacred meals became the food of Christianity's sacred meal, the Eucharist.

What do bread and wine signify? I hinted in answering the question about what is proper to bring up at the presentation of the gifts at Mass (question 47) that the symbols of bread and wine are very significant because they are the result of human manufacture. The process that we humans engage in to produce these foodstuffs has many levels of meaning, and we need to look at the process and the result to appreciate why we still use bread and wine at Mass. The baking of bread involves a series of actions that themselves are regarded as *paschal*, meaning dying and rising. (The same is true for wine. But for brevity we'll discuss bread and make an application to wine at the end.) The beginning of the process is planting and harvesting. In at least a metaphorical sense the grain of wheat first has to die (Jn 12:24) to yield rich fruit. Seed has to be planted in the ground to produce the shafts of wheat, which are themselves cut down, harvested then milled into flour. Hence even the flour itself has a paschal symbolism. Then the baking of bread requires kneading and (normally) a series of risings before it is baked and fresh bread is produced. Again the process of baking itself sustains a level of paschal symbolism. The same is true for wine: planting, harvesting grapes, crushing them into liquid, fermentation—all are involved in the "paschal" process of making the wine. My point is that these foods themselves are central symbols of paschal dying and rising and hence are most fitting to represent the Eucharist as our sharing in Christ, our food for eternal life.

Finally a word about custom. It was because bread and wine were the customary foods for Jewish ceremonial meals that Jesus used them and we follow this precedent. But it was also customary through the early Middle Ages that Christians used leavened bread at the Eucharist. And to this day it is still customary to use leavened bread in the Eastern churches for the Eucharist. The West came to use only unleavened bread because fewer and fewer people were actually receiving communion at Mass, and concern grew regarding reverence toward the eucharistic elements. Hence, it was judged best to use unleavened bread because there would be fewer crumbs that might inadvertently not be eaten and therefore reverently received. The fact that the East uses leavened bread and the West uses unleavened bread indicates a certain variety in the use of bread and represents diversity in unity. But the fact that we all use bread and wine signifies our faithfulness to what Jesus did.

51. When should the priest go to the altar and when should he leave it?

As I begin to respond to your question, I am thinking of the familiar mantra of realtors when it comes to assessing the value of a property: location, location, location. This came to mind because where and how individual parts of the Mass take place offers much to reflect on theologically. Up to now, I am sure you have noticed that I have continually referred to what the liturgy says in explaining what the Mass is. Your question invites us to realize that the location of *where* we do different parts of the Mass can often tell us something very important about that part of the Mass.

At the beginning and at the end of Mass, the priest (and deacon) reverence the altar, normally by kissing it. *The Sacramentary* then states that the priest moves to stand at the altar in order to place the bread and wine on it during the presentation of the gifts, and he leaves the altar to distribute communion. After the distribution he "may return to the chair." After a period of silence he says the prayer after communion "standing at the chair or the altar."

If you remember the Tridentine Mass, you recall that in low Masses the priest stayed at the altar for the whole Mass. In solemn Masses he went from the bench to the altar several times during the Mass. This was stipulated in the solemn Tridentine Mass and is required for every Mass because, like all other liturgies, the Mass involves movement, processions and gestures. It also emphasizes three principal locations during the Mass: the chair, the lectern (or ambo) and the altar itself. These three locations emphasize different aspects of the Mass, especially the location for proclaiming the Word at the lectern and for the proclamation of the eucharistic prayer at the altar.

52. Sometimes the priest says prayers over the bread and wine with our response, "Blessed be God forever," and sometimes he doesn't. Why?

Well, as I mentioned in answer to question 48 regarding the "offertory," one of the clearest examples of revising the Mass was the decision after Vatican II to severely reduce the number and kinds of prayers said over the bread and wine as they are placed on the altar. The committee charged with the task of revising the Mass simply took out all the prayers in the former missal. But since this was thought to be too drastic a change, the decision was made to introduce the (briefer) texts you refer to. Now technically these aren't prayers because prayers name and address God, name our need, ask that it be granted through Christ, and at the end we all say "Amen." The texts at the presentation of the gifts are acclamations acknowledging God's rule over all creation, our participation in manufacturing the bread and wine and the concluding acclamation, "Blessed be God forever." Now some have questioned the legitimacy of these acclamations because their origin is the same genre of Jewish prayers used as the basis for the eucharistic prayer itself. In fact, the very situation that those who reformed the missal wanted to resolve (because the prayers at the "offertory" resembled the Roman canon) in effect produced the same result as before, since both the eucharistic prayer and these presentation texts are from the same matrix of Jewish prayer!

The directions in the *Missal* now state that the priest takes the bread, "holding it slightly raised above the altar" (in a gesture that shows the bread to the people, not in an elaborate gesture of offering as at the final doxology and great amen) and "says inaudibly" the "Blessed are you, Lord God of all creation" text. So from the outset we learn that these texts are not meant to be heard. Hence, the issue you raise in your question concerns when you hear the prayers aloud and when you do not. But then the *Missal* states "if no offertory song is sung the priest may say the prayers in an audible voice; then the people may respond 'Blessed be God forever.'" Notice the careful use of the word "may," which again signifies that these prayers are considered relatively unimportant, especially as compared with the other prayers of the Mass: the presidential, the collect type and especially the eucharistic prayer itself. The other thing to note is that the missal is filled with directions about how the priest should celebrate the Mass and that not all prayers are to be said aloud. The fact that we hear these texts over the bread and wine as often as we do may indicate that we need to be more attentive to what the missal actually says. When you say and hear every text in the missal the result may be that the more important texts seem like all the others. There are gradations to the mass prayers. The texts at the presentation of the gifts are clearly less, not more, important than others. The very use of the term "may" means there is an option. Perhaps part of the reason is that "less is more!"

53. Why does the priest wash his hands at Mass? They certainly don't seem to be dirty.

The historical background for this rite comes (once again) from the Jewish Passover ritual. When the father of the family was about to break the blessed bread and distribute it to the gathered family and friends, he would wash his hands as a sign of purification. Hence there is a spiritual, ritual background to what was also a custom in the Roman rite.

If you recall my answer to question 45, I stated that the earliest descriptions we have of the presentation of gifts at Mass included all kinds of foodstuffs in addition to bread and wine. These foods, such as wine, cheese, oil, and fresh fruits and vegetables were brought forward at Mass so that afterward they could be distributed to the poor. (Deacons most usually did this.) You and I know what happens to our hands when we choose foods at the market and unpack those foods when we get home. So you can well imagine that the priest needed to wash his hands before handling the eucharistic gifts at the altar and at communion. The priest may also have had to wash his hands when he used incense over the eucharistic gifts. To this day, when the priest uses incense at Mass his hands may get dirty because of the charcoal and smoke. Hence the custom of washing hands had another practical meaning.

Because these practices died out (or were rarely engaged in) and also because of the sacred nature of what the priest is about to do when he prays the eucharistic prayer and consecrates the bread and wine to become the body and blood of Christ, the ritual of washing hands took on greater symbolic, spiritual value. It became a sign of interior purification and integrity of heart. Some scholars argue that the spiritual meaning came to be attached to hand washing in parts of Europe and eventually came to be the practice in Rome. In any event it is still part of the Mass and in the revised *Missal* when he washes his hands the priest says inaudibly one verse from Psalm 51: "Lord, wash away my iniquity; cleanse me from my sin."

54. The prayer over the gifts was also called the secret. Can you explain?

This is another case where terminology developed because of what occurred liturgically. The earliest evidence we have of a prayer at this part of the Mass calls it the prayer over the gifts principally because after the gifts were collected and the bread and wine were placed on the altar, there was one collect-type prayer that the priest said over them. Sometimes this prayer referred to what the church community desired as a result of their participation in the Mass. Therefore, petitions for peace, unity or forgiveness of sins were common. At other times, these prayers referred to what these gifts were as signs of our devotion to God. At still other times, these prayers linked the particular feast being celebrated with the eucharistic action, for example the sacrifice that a martyr offered in giving his or her life as that act reflected Christ's self-sacrifice as perpetuated in the Mass.

During the Middle Ages, for a variety of reasons, what was always regarded as the high point of the Mass, the proclamation of the eucharistic prayer, came to be regarded as the priest's solemn prayer, which he spoke in a very soft voice. This led to an emphasis on the "silent canon" as being very fitting because silence would connote reverence and sacredness. Thus, the prayer over the gifts came to be prayed almost silently. The reason was that it was so close to the canon and if the canon was silent and so sacred, it was a logical step to view this prayer as a silent introduction to the silent canon. Hence the way it was prayed—softly, or perhaps "secretly"—was the principal reason it came to be called the "secret."

55. What is the meaning of the prayer, "May the Lord receive the sacrifice from *your* hands…," when at other places the priest refers to "*our* sacrifice"?

Your question raises a number of important liturgical and theological issues, starting with the meaning of what the priest does at Mass when he uses plural pronouns such as "we," "our" and "us." I tell my students that the trick to understanding the Mass lies in the use of pronouns and the fact that the prayers almost always use the plural form, even when one person, whether priest or deacon, is praying them. Classically, this indicates that the Mass is always a communal action of the whole church and that even when individual persons pray, they speak for and with the whole community. Therefore the presidential prayers, especially, articulate that it is always "we" who ask this through Christ. In fact, the American bishops asked that the original phrasing of the creed, "I believe" (for *Credo in unum Deum*) be changed to "*we* believe in one God" precisely to conform to the custom of using the plural form in liturgical speech. (This observation goes back to my prior remarks about the creed itself and why it was first worded "I believe." The creed originated in the baptismal rite, in which the individual asserted boldly for all to hear that yes, indeed, I do believe. The change from Latin to the vernacular may have shocked some people because "I believe" was used instead of the usual "communal" phrases, such as, "we ask this…." So the bishops asked for this pastoral adjustment.) On a more technical level the phrase that the church uses to describe how and why it is that the priest prays for the whole church is "in the person of the church" *(in persona ecclesiae)*, which means that the prayer of the priest is always done on behalf of the whole church.

Now, getting back to your precise question, what light does this shed on other prayers that use the singular "I," or "my"? In the present missal the most obvious place where "I" is used is at the invitation to communion, when we echo the words of the centurion in the gospel of Matthew (8:8): "I am not worthy to receive you." We retain the "I" form precisely because this is a quote from the scriptures. But there are other places where the classic "we" form is not used, and the priest uses the "I" form, or we use the "my" form. For the priest, this occurs in the words he prays to himself at his communion (according to the missal) "I eat your body and drink your blood." For the people, this occurs when we use the "I confess" formula at the beginning of Mass. A little historical perspective is important here. During the Middle Ages, people came to receive the Eucharist less and less frequently, largely because of a heightened awareness of the reality of Christ's presence in the Eucharist. This led to an increased sense of personal unworthiness that inhibited reception of communion. This notion of being indeed "unworthy" led to the additon of texts in the Mass acknowledging this fact. Hence the statement, "I confess" (which was originally a prayer of the priest, not of the people) and the prayer, "I eat your body" before the priest's communion. The rationale here is that the priest had to declare his unworthiness and he did so during Mass. But these were regarded as private prayers, and were not to be confused with the public prayers, true to the nature of the liturgy, which are normally in the "we" form.

Now back to your precise question. The part of the Mass you are referring to is called the invitation to prayer, containing an explicit invitation by the priest: "Pray, brethren, that *our* (Latin: *meum ac vestrum*: literally 'mine and yours') sacrifice may be acceptable..." and the people's response: "May the Lord accept the sacrifice at your hands..." (*de manibus tuis*, literally "from your hands"). Recall here what I said in response to the previous question about the prayer over the gifts becoming the "secret." This meant that this part of the Mass was totally silent. But what was approaching was the most important part of the Mass, the consecration, during the eucharistic prayer. Hence, in the Middle Ages it was decided to insert this introduction by the priest (who turned and faced the people at this point) to indicate the importance of what was to follow and to invite the congregation's attention. The Latin phrasing *meum ac vestrum ("mine and yours")* uses the connecting term *ac* and not *et* (which literally means "and"). The meaning of the Latin term *ac* is that this is a sacrifice of the priest and people because it is a sacrifice first from the priest's hands to God and that thereby it is a sacrifice of the people too. The sense of the priest's role is as instrument of the enacting of the sacrifice for the people.

Let me summarize what I've said and apply it to this part of the Mass: The Mass prayers are always communal. Sometimes individuals are mentioned, but normally this occurs in prayers of liturgically lesser value. Also, what this (relatively minor) prayer expresses is more of an individual approach to the Mass rather than an expression of what most of the other Mass prayers state: that liturgy is always primarily the prayer of the whole church, reflected in the pronouns "we," "our" and "us."

56. Why are there three parts to the introduction to the preface and the eucharistic prayer?

Your question allows me to say a little more about the importance of the eucharistic prayer at Mass, much of which I have been hinting at all along. Namely, that the General Instruction of the Roman Missal states that the eucharistic prayer is the "center and summit of the entire celebration" (n. 54). This insight is reflected in the way it is introduced, namely the three-part dialogue you are referring to. Where does this come from? Its origins are from the Jewish custom whereby an introduction such as "The Lord be with you" would signal that an important proclamation was to follow. As early as the third century, liturgical rites found in the *Apostolic*

Tradition of Hippolytus of Rome contain the same three phrases we use today at the introduction to the eucharistic prayer. The first, "The Lord be with you," specifies what is already occurring in the Mass—that the Lord is indeed with us. As a greeting, however, it engages our attention and reminds us of what is occurring throughout the Mass and that the proclamation of the eucharistic prayer will contain a special, lyrical summary of God's mighty deeds on our behalf through salvation history. "Lift up your hearts" invites us to be especially attentive to what is to follow, not just with our minds and intellectual faculties, but in our hearts—in other words, with our whole selves. The last part, "Let us give thanks to the Lord our God," specifies exactly what is to follow: our offer of praise and thanks to God for creation and redemption. Our response here that "It is right" to do this *(dignum et iustum est)* comes from Roman legal rhetoric, which would commonly use the couplet "right and just" to signify our willingness to do what is within our competence and what we should feel responsible for. The importance of this phrase is seen in the fact that it is repeated in the next line, among the first words of the priest, and forms something of an echo of our response: "It is truly right and just." This is to say that the first words the priest says in the preface are (literally), "It is truly right and just" (the same Latin phrase plus the intensive form from the word "truly," *vere*) "that we should always and everywhere give you thanks."

What should be clear is that this introduction sets up and emphasizes the eucharistic prayer, that its phrasing is not arbitrary, and that its threefold structure indicates the high value placed on the eucharistic prayer that follows.

57. What does the term "preface" mean in relation to the term "eucharistic prayer"?

Your question asks for a theological as well as a historical response. Theologically, the preface is part of the eucharistic prayer. We are accustomed to use the term "preface" to refer to an introduction, but in the Mass the meaning of "preface" comes from the prefix *pre*, which refers to the fact that this text is a prayer "before God" and "before the congregation," meaning that what follows is proclaimed and stated before others.

What caused the separation between the preface and the eucharistic prayer offers another instance of why it is important to understand the historical evolution of the Mass. From the fifth century until Vatican II, the Roman rite had one eucharistic prayer. It was called the "*Roman* canon" because of its origins in the "Roman" tradition, the rites associated with Rome. It was called the *canon*, from the Latin term meaning "fixed," because it was used daily, and no other text replaced it. But before we go out too far on a limb, let me also say that the Roman canon, while a fixed structure, also contained sections within it that changed for a given liturgical feast or season. This practice characterizes the present missal, which has parts of the canon for Christmas, Easter and so forth. Given this fixed canon structure, it was not a surprise that the first part of the canon, which had the greatest number of variable texts, came to be called the preface because this text changed almost daily and led to the more fixed canon segments that followed. In the earliest collection of missal prayers (called the *Verona Manuscript* or the Leonine *Sacramentary*) we find over two hundred and sixty prefaces! This number diminished over time with the result that the Tridentine missal had just over a dozen. The present reform sought to offer much greater variety in the prefaces and eucharistic prayers (see questions 59 to 61). Today we have over ninety prefaces in the missal. It may not be the number the Leonine *Sacramentary* boasted, but it is clearly an important attribute of the present missal. Theologically and liturgically, today it is best to understand that preface and eucharistic prayer go together and are intrinsically connected.

58. Sometimes we sing the "holy, holy, holy" and other parts of the eucharistic prayer and sometimes we don't. Why? How important are these acclamations?

Your question is an important one especially because it indicates how the eucharistic prayer is not a monologue by the priest. In the earliest description of the structure of the Mass we have from the *First Apology* of Justin the Martyr (150) at the end of the eucharistic prayer the people sang "Amen." This conclusion was said to be a resounding and very significant affirmation of "So be it" by the whole assembly. Then, by the time we have textual evidence of the Roman canon (fifth century) we find the "holy, holy, holy" acclamation you are referring to. It was originally sung by all present and was called the *sanctus* because it began with a threefold *sanctus, sanctus, sanctus*. However, by the time the canon came to be silent, it was said by the server(s) and the priest himself, but in a very soft voice.

(As with most of their involvement in the Mass, the servers' function here was to substitute for the participation of the whole congregation.) Before the present reform of the missal, when the *sanctus* was sung, it was sung by the choir and not the assembly. Therefore, the fact that you refer to singing the "holy, holy, holy" is a good sign that the intended reform of the Mass at this point has taken place.

One of the main features of the present missal has been the restoration of the eucharistic prayer to central prominence by having the priest proclaim it aloud (or sing it) and by having the whole assembly join in three specific acclamations during it. These acclamations are the "holy, holy, holy," the memorial acclamation (one of four choices beginning with "Christ has died, Christ is risen, Christ will come again") and the final amen, sometimes called the great amen. The General Instruction of the Roman Missal states that at the end of the preface the "holy, holy, holy" acclamation follows. In answer to your precise question it is useful to quote what the Instruction says: "the congregation sings or recites the *sanctus*. The acclamation is an intrinsic part of the eucharistic prayer and all the people join with the priest in singing or reciting it" (n. 55 c).

Recall what I said at the beginning of the previous answer, namely, that the eucharistic prayer is a solemn declaration of praise and thanks for God's gifts to us of creation and redemption. Now recall the text of the *sanctus* acclamation. The first part acclaims God because "heaven and earth are full of your glory." This first part of this text is adapted from Isaiah 6:2–3, which was a common feature of Jewish liturgical prayer, especially at the synagogue service of the word at morning prayer. It is a lyrical prayer that praises God for the gift of creation. This is a central feature of Jewish liturgical prayer and our Christian liturgical experience. It is important that we not forget that we revere and acclaim a God of both creation and redemption. The second part of the acclamation, "Blessed is he who comes in the name of the Lord" from Matthew 21:9, serves as a link to this second motif of the eucharistic prayer—praising God for redemption. In some eucharistic prayers in history the praise for God's outstretched hand of redemption to Israel is summarized here; in the present missal this theme is very clear in the fourth eucharistic prayer. In all eucharistic prayers God is then praised and thanked for Christ's gracious act of redemption and all that he did for our sakes and for our salvation.

The acclamation that follows the words of institution, "This is my body/blood," is new to the Mass since Vatican II. The rationale here is that if the Mass is essentially the actualization of Christ's paschal mystery as *the* mystery of faith, therefore it would make sense to emphasize this part of the eucharistic prayer with an acclamation. Hence the "invention" of the "memorial acclamation," which term refers to its role as part of the memorial prayer (that follows) within the eucharistic prayer. We now have four choices for the text of this acclamation, all of which specify Christ's death and resurrection. One of the present texts, "Dying you destroyed our death, rising you restored our life, Lord Jesus come in glory," is particularly helpful. Why? For one thing it states very simply how Christ's paschal death and resurrection affect us: by destroying the power of death forever and by raising us to resurrection through Christ. Note how it does this by the careful use of pronouns: *our* death, *our* life. Then it also very briefly states that Christ's paschal mystery includes the second coming when "Christ will come again" in glory—something we pray for at every Eucharist. We plead for this fulfillment in this acclamation in the direct invocation: "Lord Jesus, come in glory." This acclamation is therefore a most useful expression for the assembly to use to make the eucharistic prayer its own, to ratify in song what is occurring through the priest's proclamation and action. The final doxology at the end of the eucharistic prayer, "...through him, with him..." concludes with the people's assent, the affirmation "Amen" meaning "So be it." This is the acclamation that Justin asserted was done robustly!

The General Instruction of the Roman Missal summarizes its section on the eucharistic prayer by saying that "the eucharistic prayer calls for all to listen in silent reverence, but also to take part through the acclamations for which the rite makes provision" (n. 55 h). Hence, we can say that the acclamations are the people's parts of the eucharistic prayer and should be sung or said by all present. In the previous Tridentine Mass the *sanctus* and amen were sung by the choir largely because the choir had taken over almost all of the spoken and sung means of participating in the Mass. The definite instruction of the present missal is to restore them to everyone.

In 1972 the American bishops issued the document Music in Catholic Worship, which developed from the Vatican documents on renewing liturgical music. In this document it states that the people's acclamations at the eucharistic prayer rank highest in the order of what should be sung at every Mass. The fact that you don't always sing them, but that you say them, probably indicates that this occurs at Masses when there is no music at all. This is understandable given where we have been with liturgical music after Trent. But I need to be true to all of the official instructions about music in the reformed liturgy by asserting once more that the singing of these acclamations is meant to be part of every Mass. In terms of the theology of the Mass, they deserve this emphasis because the *sanctus* summarizes the themes of the eucharistic prayer. The memorial acclamation is the people's ratification and affirmation that this prayer also enacts Christ's paschal mystery and the amen is our solemn assent to what has taken place in this prayer.

59. Why did we have one canon in the Tridentine Mass and now have nine of them?

Actually we now have ten! But first let me begin by adjusting your terminology in light of my answer to question 57. Technically, the term "Roman canon" refers to the fixed text of the eucharistic prayer that has been in use in the Catholic Church since the fifth century. Technically speaking, it does not refer to the other eucharistic prayers now in use. But, at the risk of sounding like a logic professor, I need to say that all the other prayers, as well as the canon, are called eucharistic prayers precisely because they are prayers of thanks and praise ("Eucharist" means thanksgiving).

Now why do we have additional texts? One of the most important persons who influenced this particular change in the Mass is Cipriano Vagaggini, who wrote *The Canon of the Mass and Liturgical Reform*, which describes the rationale for this change. In the first part of the book he summarizes many of the strengths of the Roman canon: its emphasis on Christ, its emphasis on the apostles and saints of the Catholic Church, its emphasis on intercession and what we gain from joining in the Mass, and so forth. But then he goes on to evaluate the single Roman canon in light of the wealth of other eucharistic prayers that liturgical history has given us from other rites. Here he notes, among other things, the almost complete lack of any mention of the Holy Spirit in the canon, its (perhaps) overemphasis on intercession and the fact that the Roman rite's precedent for variety in the prefaces could well substantiate a move toward adding new eucharistic prayers to the Mass—for the sake of variety, especially if it is a prayer that will be proclaimed in the vernacular. These suggestions were taken very seriously, and the result was to make some slight editing adjustments to the canon and to add three "new" eucharistic prayers to the

missal. I put "new" in quotes because these are really not new compositions. What we now call the second eucharistic prayer is actually from the
document I quoted in answer to question 56, the *Apostolic Tradition* of
Hippolytus of Rome. This text was offered as a model for a newly
ordained bishop to use at his ordination Eucharist. The text as we have it
in the missal has been slightly adjusted, and the *sanctus* acclamation has
been added, but its sum and substance are from the third century in Rome.
The third eucharistic prayer was put together by Father Vagaggini himself
from some material from North Africa. The fourth eucharistic prayer is
certainly the longest and most embellished theologically. Its source is the
Eastern liturgical tradition, and its most important influence is from the
Apostolic Constitutions from Antioch. This prayer has its own preface,
which cannot be substituted by any other preface. The reason? The next
time you hear it at Mass, notice that the praise of God for creation is the
dominant theme of the preface, which motif continues in the first part of
the eucharistic prayer that follows the *sanctus*. Since all the other prefaces
acclaim and describe facets of Christ's redemption as motives for praising
God, if we were to use any one of them this theology would jar with the
next part of eucharistic prayer four, regarding creation and God's covenant
relationship with Israel ("again and again you offered a covenant").

That gives us four. Then what happened? After the publication of the
Directory for Masses with Children, it was judged useful to compose
eucharistic prayers that would be more suitable for children's comprehension. This led to the publication of three eucharistic prayers for children. A
chief feature of these three prayers is that in addition to the three eucharistic acclamations we have just talked about (in answer to question 58), they
have added shorter acclamations interspersed throughout the prayer as a
way of keeping the children focused on the eucharistic action by singing
them. In the first of the eucharistic prayers for Masses with children, this
acclamation separates the two sections of the *sanctus* and makes them into
two acclamations. Then the entire *sanctus* is sung at the usual place. In the
second and third of these prayers a single-line acclamation runs throughout the prayer. Choices for this include: "Glory to God in the highest,"
"Hosannah in the highest," "Jesus has given his life for us," and "We
praise you, we bless you, we thank you."

Then, in preparation for the holy year of renewal and reconciliation
in 1975, Pope Paul VI asked that two additional prayers be prepared on the
theme of reconciliation. Now in the interests of full disclosure, I should

point out that there was some debate at that time regarding whether there should be additional eucharistic prayers. The argument against adding prayers was that we should let the seven prayers then in use be appropriated and assimilated fully since, after all, this was the first time the Roman Church had any prayers other than the single Roman canon. In addition, the sense was that the eucharistic prayer should become so well known that people would welcome its familiar cadences, phrases and images. Pope Paul VI, without negating any of this reasoning, still judged that the holy year theme of renewal and reconciliation was so important—and so intrinsic to the church's life—that the addition of two prayers was warranted. They were published in vernacular languages in six months.

The most recent eucharistic prayer to be added to the missal originally came from Switzerland. It was composed as a prayer to be used in that country to prepare for a national meeting (called the Swiss Synod). Then it was translated into Italian, and has been used for over a decade in Italy. The American bishops received permission from Rome to use it as part of our missal. It has the (rather awkward) title, "Eucharistic Prayer for Masses for Various Needs and Occasions." The text is really a collection of separate parts of a prayer, with four prefaces (entitled "The Church on the Way to Unity," "God Guides the Church on the Way to Salvation," "Jesus, The Way to the Father," and "Jesus, The Compassion of God"). The missal states that the priest choose one of these prefaces as well as the intercessory prayer in the eucharistic prayer corresponding to the theme of the preface. In a sense, this variety and flexibility reflects the origins and present text of the Roman canon—"fixed" in the sense of containing the same structure but varying within itself.

60. Somehow the new eucharistic prayers sound different from the Roman canon. And, in fact, I almost never hear the Roman canon anymore. Can you explain this?

Let me answer your second question first because it explains why new eucharistic prayers were added after Vatican II. In his work, *The Canon of the Mass and Liturgical Reform*, Father Cipriano Vagaggini noted that a possible defect of the Roman canon was its lack of a cohesive structure and unity of ideas. (I say "possible defect" because I do not want to seem to judge out-of-hand a prayer that has lasted the test of time and was used throughout the Roman Church from the fifth through the twentieth century!) But the fact that it is a collection of variable parts had the down side of seeming to be a less than cohesive prayer, especially when compared with eucharistic prayers from other sources, particularly Eastern ones. I suspect that this lack of cohesion in the canon, especially when compared with the new prayers, is the reason why priests usually choose the new texts. I would like to suggest, however, that the canon be used especially on the special feasts when specific parts of the prayer are included for that day, for example, Christmas, Epiphany, Easter and so forth.

Now to the broader question of the differences between the canon and the new prayers. The story behind the story of the need for new prayers (documented amply in Father Vagaggini's book, largely because he was in charge of the committee that did this work) is that liturgical scholars in the past century discovered a wealth of eucharistic prayers that have been used over the course of centuries, especially in the Eastern churches. This enabled scholars to study manuscripts and collections of texts and see that, in fact, the eucharistic prayer could have some different or additional elements than those found in the Roman canon. Because of this textual evidence of variety, the study group charged with adapting the canon and adding prayers set about its work on the basis of sound historical discoveries and scientific methods. Now back to your question. Yes, the structure of the new texts is different. The fact that at least one of the new eucharistic prayers is shorter than the canon (eucharistic prayer II), that they have a logical structure and that they clearly emphasize the role of the Holy Spirit makes them certainly worthy of frequent use. Let me outline this structure and make some comments on it.

According to the General Instruction of the Roman Missal, the chief elements that make up the eucharistic prayer are: thanksgiving, acclamation, epiclesis, institution, anamnesis, offering, intercessions and final doxology (n. 55). "Thanksgiving" refers to the nature of the prayer as a solemn declaration of praise and thanks. It is especially prominent in the preface, where a specific aspect of God's work of salvation is noted. (For example, one of the Easter prefaces echoes the memorial acclamation and states: "Dying you destroyed our death, rising you restored our life." Thus, at Easter we praise God for Christ's paschal mystery and for our becoming sharers in it, especially since this participation is renewed in the liturgy.) The second element, acclamation, refers to the church's joining the praise of the "angels and saints" as we sing the "holy, holy, holy." The other acclamations during the eucharistic prayer include the memorial acclamation after the words of institution, and the great amen after the final doxology. (Recall my response to question 58; also, you might want to look ahead to question 84.)

Now for us in the Roman Catholic Church, the next part of the prayer is new—the epiclesis. This is the element that Father Vagaggini did not find in the canon and that needed to be restored to our liturgical prayer. "Epiclesis" refers to an explicit invocation that God, through the power of the Holy Spirit, consecrate the gifts we present at the Eucharist. In most eucharistic prayer texts in liturgical history, this prayer explicitly invokes the power of the Holy Spirit. Therefore, in the second eucharistic prayer we find the words, "Let your Spirit come upon these gifts to make them holy." In addition, another theme of the epiclesis prayer is for the church's unity. Hence, in that same prayer we have the text, "May all of us who share in the body and blood of Christ be brought together in unity by the Holy Spirit." These two themes—transformation of the gifts and the unity of the church—are classic in the liturgical tradition of the churches, are specific to the epiclesis and reflect the crucial role that the Holy Spirit plays in the action of the Eucharist. Hence, these parts of every eucharistic prayer added to the Mass are an extremely important addition to our prayer.

The next element of the eucharistic prayer is the institution narrative and consecration. As I am sure you have noticed, when the priest gets to this part of all the eucharistic prayers he begins to use the words of Jesus from the Last Supper: "...take this all of you...this is my body...blood." In the structure of the eucharistic prayer these words take on an even greater significance as the wider framework of the Last Supper is recalled. Our attention is thus drawn to the wider canvas and not just to the text, "...this is my body...blood." The fact that this section is called the institution narrative and consecration signals an emphasis on the words and gestures that recall the Last Supper when Jesus instituted this sacramental action.

The next section, with the name "anamnesis," needs a bit of background to understand. Literally, this term is a transliteration of the Greek word for memorial. But the kind of memorial indicated here comes from the Jewish and scriptural understanding of what "memorial" means. For the Jew of Jesus' day (and our own times), the notion of remembrance is not merely a mental exercise. Rather "memorial" means that we invoke God's action and presence, and ask that it be active among us now. The phrase of the rabbis, "To remember is to give life, to forget is to let die," is a good way of appreciating what "anamnesis" means. When we engage in a prayer of remembrance, God does something for us. When we ask God to "forget" something, like sin, then it has no existence. You can see, therefore, how important this part of the eucharistic prayer is, especially the command, "...do this in memory of me." We come to Mass to *do* what Jesus commanded. We don't just come to think about the way it was in Palestine in his lifetime. Rather, what we are doing is commemorating—literally "remembering together"—what God has done through Christ, and in the remembering, experiencing it as fully and deeply as is humanly possible. It makes sense, therefore, that the church would want to emphasize this part of the prayer with the new memorial acclamations (which normally precede this part of the prayer, but which in the eucharistic prayers for masses with children, follow the memorial prayer itself).

The next section, the offering, explicitates what we do in the Mass—we offer Christ to the Father and, at the same time, surrender ourselves to God through, with and in Christ. This is the classic place where the language of "offer" and "offering" is found in the Mass, not at what we used to call the offertory. (For more on this, see question 48.) The next section, the intercessions, was admittedly a chief feature of the Roman canon. With the revision of the missal and the addition of the new eucharistic prayers, these intercessions were set within a larger prayer with several other themes. This means that while we do acknowledge and name what we ask God for in the Mass, we don't make this so central that other aspects of the prayer are diminished, especially praise and thanks for the mighty acts of salvation. The dynamic in this prayer (as well as in all liturgical prayer) is a balance between praise and petition, a balance between thanks and request.

The final doxology concludes these prayers. This is a very important example of the relationship of the church to the Trinity. In the final doxology, we assert that all we have done is through, with and in Christ. We also assert that all that we do in the Mass—especially offering our praise and thanks—is "in the unity of the Holy Spirit." Now this phrase deserves some unpacking! On one level, the more obvious one, this phrase refers to the Holy Spirit, the third person of the Trinity. But on another, less obvious but nonetheless very important level, this phrase refers to the community that makes up the church. You see, "in the unity of the Holy Spirit" refers to the members of the church that, in their coming together in unity, make up the praying church at the Eucharist. Hence, at the end of the eucharistic prayer what we have is a very fitting combination of factors that really summarize what the eucharistic prayer is all about: naming the persons of the Trinity and naming the church as the community of believers that gathers for this unique act of offering thanks and praise as we remember Christ's paschal death and resurrection.

I'm sure you can now see why you have a different sense when you hear the new eucharistic prayers that mirror this outline most concretely. To help you get even more out of this part of the Mass, I'd suggest your reading over and meditating on the texts of the eucharistic prayers. The more we know the logical flow and the wording of what we pray at this part of the Mass, the more it will become what it is meant to be: "…the center and summit of the entire celebration" (General Instruction, n. 54).

61. I don't hear a lot about the consecration. I was taught that it was the most important part of the Mass. What happened?

For anyone who was accustomed to the Mass before Vatican II, your question resonates very well. Indeed, we were taught that the consecration was the most important part of the Mass. This was because of the Reformation controversies and our need to insist that our theology and practice of the Eucharist emphasized the real presence of Christ as much as possible. Now that those pressures have lifted, we have come to appreciate other aspects of the Mass as important as well, such as the whole Liturgy of the Word, receiving communion every time we go to Mass and the proclamation of the whole eucharistic prayer. At the same time, as I indicated in response to the previous question, historical scholarship deepened our knowledge about what was contained in eucharistic prayers that were not just the same type as the Roman canon. It was this rigorous historical research that revealed the very important place that the epiclesis played in the text and the proclamation of this prayer. Recall that the epiclesis is a prayer of invocation for the transformation of bread and wine into the body and blood of Christ, and a prayer for ever more complete and full unity of the church. Now that this part of the eucharistic prayer is an important part of nine out of ten of the eucharistic prayers in the present missal, it is clear that we need to take this prayer seriously as an essential part of the whole Mass. Now if we Western (Roman) Catholics look at this text through an Eastern lens, we would see how logical it was for some Eastern theologians to state that it was at the epiclesis that the bread and wine became the body and blood of Christ. After all to state, "...let your Spirit come upon these gifts" is a pretty strong assertion that transformation is to occur now.

On the other hand, if you were a Catholic theologian through the Middle Ages and experienced the canon without an explicit epiclesis invoking the Holy Spirit, then it would be logical that you might argue (as most did!) that when the priest says the words of Jesus, "...this is my body, this is my blood" the bread and wine become Christ's body and blood. Now that the epiclesis has been restored as an element of the eucharistic prayer, we can assert that perhaps the best way to understand *when* the consecration happens is during the eucharistic prayer as a whole, especially from the epiclesis asking that the gifts be transformed through the institution narrative and the anamnesis to the second epiclesis for church unity. This enables us not to have to make an either/or decision at the epiclesis or the institution narrative. It also underscores the emphasis in the General Instruction of the Roman Missal, which continually adds the description "institution narrative" to the term "consecration." This phrasing is the church's way of saying, "Appreciate what this whole text is," and not just to look at what happens as a result of its being prayed.

Lastly, as one liturgical directive of the importance of the epiclesis *and* the institution narrative *and* the anamnesis, let's take a look at the directions for a concelebrated Mass (when one or more priests assist at Mass with the presiding priest or bishop). As you probably have noticed at these Masses, when the presiding priest/bishop begins the epiclesis for the transformation of the bread and wine, all the other priests extend their hands (with palms down as a gesture invoking the Spirit) and say the whole central part of the eucharistic prayer through the end of the anamnesis with the presiding priest. This is a rubrical directive to support what I have urged here. Namely, that we don't regard "...this is my body...blood" as a formula to convert bread and wine into Christ's body and blood, but that we see this part of the eucharistic prayer in relation to the prayer as a whole as the center of the whole celebration.

Let me now add one observation from the church's prayer here about the role of the priest. Whatever view one might have taken historically about when the transformation takes place, one thing is sure: that in the epiclesis the phrase "let your Spirit come upon these gifts" or any variation of it, is a theologically significant assertion that whatever we do in the liturgy is always done through the power of the Spirit—not on our own. Similarly, when the priest uses the words of Jesus from the Last Supper, "...this is my body...blood," he is reminded that these words are not his; they are Christ's. This is to say that this part of the eucharistic prayer is different from what occurs before because up to this point the phrasing in the priest's text has been in the name of the church and an address to God, such as, "We come to you Father...." Here, at the institution narrative, by using the words of Christ, he reminds us that the transformation is not up to the priest himself. Rather, it is up to the very person of Christ, whose words and actions he recalls at this part of the Mass. But again, the power to consecrate comes from Christ's words. The priest's power, in either case, is vicarious in the best sense of that term. The priest speaks and acts in the name and person of Christ—not on his own. This is a humbling reminder of who the priest is and of the overwhelming power of the Trinity at work in the action of the Mass.

The last thing I'd like to say about your question regarding the consecration is that in the reformed Mass much greater emphasis is now placed on the people's reception of communion. This shifts the emphasis away from the post-Reformation triad: offertory, consecration and communion (of the priest). This made for a valid Mass. In a technical sense, it still does. But the communion of the priest leads to the communion of all the assembly gathered for Mass. In other words, the consecration of the elements occurs so that we can share in the transformed eucharistic gifts—Christ's body and blood. Perhaps another reason why you don't hear much about the consecration is that when we Catholics emphasized it, few of us actually received communion. Now that most of us receive communion every time we celebrate the Mass, it would make sense that we emphasize the act of sharing in communion as an (equally?) important element of the Mass. After all, the purpose of the Mass is our participation (taking part) in Christ's act of salvation for us and the consecration of the elements makes this possible through eucharistic communion.

62. You seem to be placing a lot of emphasis on the action of the Holy Spirit in the eucharistic prayer and in the Mass in general. Can you really justify this since the Holy Spirit was only mentioned at the very

end of the Roman canon and therefore was not central to the Mass before Vatican II?

Your question is a very significant one, and this topic has been very much at the forefront of recent liturgical writings. In fact, one of the reasons why I answered the previous two questions at some length is that the emphasis placed on the Holy Spirit in the texts of the prayers of the present Mass (and therefore the understanding of the Mass) is nothing short of revolutionary.

But first of all I'd like to clear up something that may be behind your question; that is, whether this emphasis on the Spirit is an indirect way of saying that the former missal was wrong. Or, as some people put it today, if the Roman canon was *the* eucharistic prayer for fifteen centuries, who are we to change it? (I am reminded here of my answer to question 18 regarding the notion of a "new" Mass.) The best simple answer I can give comes from a document at the very beginning of the present missal, the Apostolic Constitution, written by Pope Paul VI, authorizing the publication and use of the new missal. This is more than a legal document insisting that the missal be used. It is a very helpful summary of the chief features of the revised Mass. In this relatively brief text, the pope asserts that "no one should think…that this revision of *The Roman Missal* has come out of nowhere. The progress in liturgical studies during the last four centuries has certainly prepared the way…[and that] ancient sources have been discovered and liturgical formularies of the Eastern Church have been studied." It is this contribution of recent liturgical scholarship, especially the influence of Eastern texts, that has enabled the church to put together the riches of this new missal. The pope recalled the words of Pope Pius V, who endorsed the Tridentine missal (in 1570) and stated that the study of ancient manuscripts "helped greatly in the correction of *The Roman Missal.*" In a sense then, the publication of both the Tridentine and the present missal demonstrates that at both times the missal then in use was corrected by the new missal. Finally, with regard to the addition of new eucharistic prayers, Paul VI stated that "the chief innovation in the reform concerns the eucharistic prayer." From these authoritative statements I would argue that the addition of emphasis on the power and role of the Holy Spirit in the Mass is a legitimate advancement in the Catholic Church's prayer that is based on traditional sources and is a most legitimate advance to enhance our liturgical prayer.

Now with regard to your asking whether what we prayed in the Tridentine missal is to be considered "wrong," I guess I'd like to use the term "inadequate." This allows for the pride of place given to the Tridentine missal over the centuries, and to the canon over a thousand years older than the Tridentine missal. Just as the Tridentine missal improved what came before it, so the missal of Paul VI, officially endorsed by the highest church authority and based on the liturgical scholarship of our day, helps the present church to benefit from recent liturgical study and to achieve a less inadequate set of prayers for the Mass. (I say "less inadequate" because we will never ever achieve a "perfect" Mass in this life!) In addition, the emphasis we now place on the epiclesis in the eucharistic prayer and on the Holy Spirit in general cannot but help in ecumenical relations among all the churches—East and West. The new missal is liturgically and theologically normative. From now on we can develop a more and more adequate theology of the Mass from the richness of its prayers, especially those that point to the active role of the Holy Spirit in the Mass.

Much of what I have consistently argued in this book is based on what the liturgy says and by this means to unpack what the liturgy means. The new eucharistic prayers are normative and offer a great deal to reflect on in order to understand what we do when we celebrate the Mass. The new missal simply offers much that is new and that can be used to develop our understanding of what the Mass really means.

63. Sometimes our priest says something different in the eucharistic prayer and in some other parts of the Mass. Is this allowed?

Let me begin by making some comments on where the eucharistic prayer came from in Jewish practice, because this may help us understand the notion of variety within a prayer that is sometimes legitimate and sometimes not. The religious customs of Judaism placed great value on sharing meals together with family and friends in faith. During those meals there would always be some public declaration as to why they would gather, and normally such statements included thanking God for liberation and sanctification: for example, liberation from the bondage of slavery in Egypt and the hope and promise of coming into the presence of the all holy God. The structure of such a blessing prayer included three things. The first part was a solemn declaration to "bless" God (Hebrew root for this is *berakah*, translated as, "Blessed are you Lord God"). The second part was a declaration of thanks, elaborating on why we acknowledged God in this way. The third part was a supplication, asking that the God who was blessed and thanked would continue to shower grace and favor on the chosen people. The name for this particular prayer form is (in Hebrew) the *birkat-ha-mazon*. Now the structure of this prayer form is fixed, but its content was not so fixed. It was the responsibility of the one presiding to elaborate or embellish on this structure, most especially the second part. It is this precedent or custom of elaborating within a fixed prayer form that gave rise in early Christianity for this to be the custom at Christian eucharists or meal fellowship. Therefore in his *Apostolic Tradition*, what Hippolytus gave to the newly ordained bishop as a eucharistic prayer was a fairly detailed outline—but it was an outline that he could elaborate on in light of a given feast or occasion. This precedent for variety within a structured text gave rise to the custom in the Roman rite of having many prefaces for the Roman canon. This is also the precedent for the fact that the canon itself contained varied and variable parts within it. (I suspect this precedent in the Roman canon gave rise to the fact that the recently approved Eucharistic Prayer for Various Needs and Occasions is a prayer with four prefaces and four intercessory sections to the single prayer.)

Now, back to your question about the priest saying "something different" in the eucharistic prayer. Clearly he has innumerable options for the preface that he can choose, and sometimes I suspect this can seem to be different from what is customary. But this is perfectly legitimate.

At the risk of becoming too fussy (nobody ever likes a "fussy liturgist"—and probably with good reason!), let me offer a general comment and two examples of "something different" that I have heard at Masses. But first let me make the general observation that when it comes to all the texts of the liturgy, we must be very respectful of what they say because they are intended to structure a ritual of prayer that is spoken and also personal, a prayer that relies on the texts but also goes beyond the texts to foster deep, interior communion with God. When those parts of the language of the liturgy that are meant to foster this kind of deeper prayer are changed, this can disrupt what ought to be going on "under" the text. So, all things being equal, I'd be slow to change ritual texts very much at all. Now let me turn to two examples.

The first is when the priest changes a text, such as "The Lord *is* with you" instead of "The Lord be with you," or "Let us *continue our* prayer" rather than "Let us pray." Now both of these interpolations have some merit. After all, by the time of the gospel or the eucharistic prayer, we have already acknowledged the Lord's presence and action among us. Hence, to assert that "the Lord is with" us sounds legitimate. The problem, however, is that this and other similar phrases (like "let us pray") constitute what I like to call ritual language. These are key phrases in the Mass when the priest uses agreed upon terminology in order to invite the assembly's particular attention. To change them can invite ritual dislocation or at least some confusion among the people.

The second example concerns the change some priests make during the eucharistic prayer over the bread and cup. The text states that Jesus gave them to the *disciples*. However, some priests change this to "his friends." Technically, I would say that this is not a desirable change because there is a wealth of meaning behind the term "disciple." I am thinking here of the powerful testimony of faith from the Lutheran pastor Dietrich Bonhoeffer during the Second World War entitled, *The Cost of Discipleship*. I am also thinking that the gospel of St. Matthew is really a manual for what it means to be a disciple; after all, the Greek term for "Matthew" literally means "disciple." And at the very end of that gospel Jesus commands the eleven disciples (Mt 28:16) to go forth and "make disciples" (vs. 19). These examples would lead me not to change this term because I would interpret the Eucharist here as the food to make us disciples less imperfect and more faithful followers of Jesus. At the same time, however, I'd like to point out that in the eucharistic prayers for Masses with children, instead of the word "disciples" these prayers use the term "friends." Now it is obvious that "friends" has been used here to suit the comprehension of children. But it is also clear that the term is not the same as "disciple" and that "disciple" carries a great deal more theological weight. However, given the fact that there are three eucharistic prayers suitable for children's comprehension, then we might well look at the use of "friends" as an example of intimacy, friendship and meal fellowship. The background here is the fact that in Judaism when one shared a meal at table, one affirmed the most intimate of relationships with others. (Hence the depth of Judas's betrayal, which was executed by one who shared a meal at table with Jesus.) The use of "friends" might well be explained in these Masses with children to underscore one of the aspects of every Mass—an intimate union with God through the action of the Mass. Clearly, the customary usage in the Roman rite at the institution narrative is usually "disciples," but sometimes it can be "friends," which variation is in the text of the Roman rite itself. If the priest changes "disciples" to "friends" at Mass, I would think that he wants to stress the intimacy of what is occurring. In this case I'd say let it go and appreciate that many terms in the liturgy have a number of very legitimate meanings.

64. Doesn't the Latin say that Christ's blood was shed for "many"? Why does our translation say "all"? And didn't it originally say "all men"? I'm confused.

The question you raise has been the subject of much debate from the beginning of experiencing the Mass in the vernacular. Some groups within the church chose this phrase as an example of heresy in the "new" Mass because of this translation. You are quite correct in observing that in both the former missal and the present Latin order of Mass, the text of the eucharistic prayers contains the phrase *pro multis effundetur*. This is from the Last Supper account in the gospel of Matthew (26:28). The literal translation is "for many," and you will find this in the standard translations of the New Testament. However, the more accurate way to translate any foreign language is to study the thought world from which phrases and words derive, especially to see whether there are terms behind the terms that need to be explained and explored for the sake of accurate translation.

Let me offer an example that ties what I have been saying about this part of the Mass with the observation of American holidays. Every year on the last Monday of May, we Americans celebrate Memorial Day, when we honor those who gave their lives in war for our freedom. It is a day of recalling to mind and heart those beloved dead who gave the supreme sacrifice for our country. Most of us appreciate this as the origin and meaning of this special civil holiday. However, if you were to take that same term "memorial" and put it back into the vocabulary of biblical times, you would soon discover that it meant a communal liturgical action whereby we invoked God's gracious favor on our behalf in light of the covenant. We invoke God's activity among us now, the very same gracious action that the God of the covenant gave to all our ancestors in the faith. Also, the sense of chronological time is collapsed in the Hebraic notion of memorial because it includes past, present and future all at the same time! We invoke God's blessings in the present on the basis of past marvelous deeds, and we look to their fulfillment in the kingdom of heaven. Similarly, when we use the biblical phrase asking God to "forget" our sins, we beg God's mercy to take them away as though they had no existence. Obviously we are not asking God to engage in a mental activity—we are asking God to do something for us here and now. Now that's a lot of baggage for the simple word "memorial." But we need to understand this rich term with its many meanings so that we can more accurately translate it liturgically and appreciate its theological depth.

The same thing is true for the term *pro multis*. The Latin here relies on the Greek, and the Greek phrase is *peri pollon*, meaning (literally) for the many as opposed to a few. But what is behind each of these languages is the Semitic understanding that "many" may seem to exclude some people, whereas in actuality it means every person except Jesus himself. Hence, the translation should be for "all" and not "many" where "many" can mean a few.

Your other point concerns the first stage of translations into English when this phrase was first translated "for all men." After a few years of usage, especially in light of increased emphasis on using language in contemporary speech that was as inclusive of all persons as possible, what emerged was the sense that "for all men" could appear to be exclusive of women. Now this was never intended. Just as the term "mankind" was not meant to exclude women, but the better rendering today is "humankind" to get beyond any unnecessary debate and confusion, so our American bishops thought it best to ask the Vatican for permission to eliminate "men" as the text over the eucharistic cup. This occurred in 1980.

65. What are the correct postures during the eucharistic prayer?

Talk about a controversial question today! Allow me to begin with some ideas about what gestures mean at the Mass and some historical observations on how they evolved over the centuries. Then I'll tackle the state of the question in America today.

One of the principles I use to teach my students about liturgy is that all liturgical prayer is *enacted ritual*. By this I mean that it is fundamentally an action, an event, an experience of salvation. It is not an idea or the process of thinking about salvation. It is God's saving presence and sanctifying action made real for us here and now. It is also a ritual in the sense that what we do in liturgy is structured, and in being structured it is familiar. In other words, we know how to participate by words, gestures, actions because they don't change. Now one of the reasons why I find the phrase "enacted ritual" useful is that this phrase betrays the fact that all who participate in the liturgy do so as humans—with minds, hearts and *bodies*. Our bodily actions, gestures and processions at Mass all reflect the fact that we are enfleshed human beings, and that we use our bodies at Mass to reflect just who we are. The way we act in human life, through speech, feelings, gestures and movement is the way we act in liturgy. We use all our human faculties in the liturgy in such a way that the liturgy respects who we are as humans and, in fact, emphasizes who we are as enfleshed human beings, because the way we honor God is through the very gifts God gave us—body, mind and heart.

Now, when you apply this to the Mass, what is clear is that the way we use our bodies reflects the way we look at ourselves before God. What we do in liturgy makes a theological statement. Therefore, it is important to understand what believers in generations before us thought about the Mass as they engaged in its various ritual gestures. When we learn, for example, that the earliest Christians through the early Middle Ages stood for the eucharistic prayer, we need to look at their teaching about the Eucharist to discover the relationship between posture and theology. In fact, there was a harmony between standing as a sign of attention, respect and (more theologically) as a sign that we have risen with Christ as a resurrected, redeemed people and the theology of the Eucharist that was an act of the pilgrim church raising minds, hearts and bodies in communal praise and thanksgiving. Sometimes standing was accompanied with raising hands in the prayer position called *orans* (Latin for "praying"). Hence, in these centuries standing and raising hands at the eucharistic prayer signified the attitude that the church was on its way to the kingdom, and that the Mass was a time for the whole community to join in ritual words and gestures in order to praise and thank God together.

By the time of the Middle Ages, we see certain shifts in theology as well as the postures people adopted at Mass. Beginning in the ninth century, theologians began to debate about what the Eucharist was and how best to describe the change from bread and wine into the body and blood of Christ. At the same time, laypeople began to revere the host and chalice with gestures of reverence. So did the priest. Hence, we find more attention given to describe what the eucharistic species of consecrated bread and wine was and the positive effects it would give to us. More and more the canon came to be recited softly, then eventually it was said in silence.

At this time the ritual gestures of the priest developed to show reverence to the consecrated bread and wine—namely, he would genuflect before them and eventually would raise them up for all to see. (In fact, the main reason why people wanted to see the host and chalice was that they no longer received communion regularly at Mass and so felt that this substitute, called ocular communion, would at least satisfy their spirituality, even when they didn't receive communion.) What is important about these gestures is that they also reflect the way humans communicate (holding the host/chalice for people to see and the act of seeing by the people). This custom led to the rubrics in the Tridentine missal that the laypeople would kneel for most of the Mass. By then, the emphasis was placed on it as the unbloody sacrifice of Calvary, which we were privileged to experience, as demonstrated by our kneeling through most of the Mass. Because the Eucharist was so "awesome," and people watched it as spectators from the Middle Ages on, it is no surprise that great emphasis was placed on kneeling as a sign of adoration.

Now, let me make a distinction here between gestures during the eucharistic prayer at Mass and gestures at other times. We have evidence that even when people stood for the eucharistic prayer in the early church, they would bow or prostrate themselves at other times at certain liturgies, specifically on Good Friday when they venerated the cross of Christ. This precedent then led to the custom of bowing before the Eucharist when people venerated it outside of the Mass. Therefore, we need to keep in mind that some gestures that are fitting for devotion outside of Mass may not be fitting for the Mass itself, principally because devotions are to the eucharistic species reserved for communion and adoration, whereas the postures assumed at Mass should reflect the theology of the eucharistic action.

This leads finally to the present state of the reform of the liturgy. The General Instruction of the Roman Missal states that the people should stand for most of the Mass but "should kneel *(genuflectant)* at the consecration, unless prevented by lack of space, large numbers of people present, or some other reasonable cause" (n. 21). Now let's put this direction in relation to the theology of the restored Mass. Clearly, the revised texts of the prayers at Mass reflect an emphasis *both* on the Mass as an action in which we participate and as Christ's sacrifice given to us. The very fact that the second eucharistic prayer (from Hippolytus in the third century) states "we thank you for counting us worthy to stand here and serve you" is an indication that standing as a posture of the pilgrim church is desirable. Also, if the emphasis on the Mass now is toward fostering our relationships with one another in community and sharing the Eucharist in communion, then we have added the gesture of processing to communion as an important ritual gesture for the whole community.

But what happened to the missal's instruction about standing and kneeling/genuflecting at the consecration only? Well, this is another instance of "When in Rome do what the Romans do," a principle that reflects much of what the church does throughout the world, which is not always uniform. Because of the phrasing of the General Instruction of the Roman Missal (n. 21), namely, "unless other provision is made" and "some reasonable cause," the decision about posture during the eucharistic prayer was left to the bishops of each country to implement. When the new missal was published, the bishops' conferences of Belgium, the Netherlands, France and the French sector of Canada opted for standing throughout the eucharistic prayer. The bishops of Spain and Italy adopted the description literally. This is why to this day in the major basilicas in Rome (e.g., St. Peter's) you never find kneelers, and that people stand for the eucharistic prayer, kneel at the consecration and resume standing for the memorial acclamation. The American bishops decided not to follow the missal's prescriptions but rather to follow a practice that had been customary for weekdays in Advent, Lent and other fast days from the Tridentine rite, namely, to kneel from the *sanctus* until after the great amen. In the only quasi-official commentary I know of that described why the bishops did what they did, what seemed to have emerged was a pastoral concern voiced by many people that they were disturbed by some of the liturgical changes after Vatican II. Thus, it was judged wise to allow the customary practice to remain in place. Some may call this expedience. But at least the majority of the bishops judged this to be pastorally wise and prudent. However, even in the United States this is not the norm for the whole country—as is evident from your own question. Some bishops have used the same phrases from the missal regarding "other provision" and "reasonable cause" to permit standing during the eucharistic prayer in their dioceses.

To conclude, I'd like to add a personal observation on the variations in practice that I experience as a priest at the eucharistic prayer. When I concelebrated Mass for some three years in a Benedictine monastery that ran a college, the posture adopted by the assembly was to stand; some people chose to kneel at the consecration only. My experience of that ritual gesture of standing was that it enabled people to be engaged in the eucharistic prayer in a special way. It captured their minds and hearts as the prayer of praise and thanks of a pilgrim church in a way that is not always common when people kneel for this prayer. In most parishes where I now celebrate Mass, I note a distinct change in attention and focus when people kneel after the "holy, holy, holy." What happens often when they kneel is that they bow their heads in reverence and adoration and seem to be less engaged in the words and action of the eucharistic prayer and the eucharistic action itself. My pastoral experience would side with the custom of following *The Roman Missal* as it is; in this instance I think the American custom deserves to be revisited.

66. I have read that we have taken the sacrifice out of the Mass. Is this true? Don't the eucharistic prayers refer to the sacrifice of the Mass?

My sense is that the rhetoric about taking the sacrifice out of the Mass really is a way for some people to complain that the Mass is not the way it was. No it isn't, and for good reasons (many of which I've already argued here!). What I'd like to suggest is that the present missal seeks to combine the notions of meal, eucharistic action and sacrament with what was the predominant emphasis in the previous missal, namely, that of the Mass as a sacrifice. The fact that the former offertory prayers were severely reduced in number and the gestures almost eliminated may cause some to view the sacrificial aspect of the Mass as diminished. In addition, the fact that the priest normally faces us during the Mass can emphasize our visual appreciation of the Mass as a sacred, ritual meal, as opposed to the priest not facing us and our watching for the elevation (as in the Tridentine Mass). But I'd like to turn the tables here and offer the observation that in fact the new missal places *more* emphasis on the sacrificial aspect of the Mass at the words of institution than the former missal did. Let me explain.

In the Tridentine missal the consecration formula for the priest was the words, "This is my body." (For those of us old enough to remember the Latin, especially us servers, we heard *hoc est enim corpus meum*.) In the present missal, this text has been expanded in all the eucharistic prayers added since Vatican II to read, "This is my body which will be given up for you." The scripture sources for both of these texts are the accounts of the Last Supper in the gospels. The source for the text in the Tridentine missal was Matthew 26:26, and for the present missal the source is Luke

22:19. The principal reason offered as to why the new missal contains the added phrase "given for you" is that it emphasizes Christ's sacrificial death and resurrection commemorated in the Eucharist for us. The declaration, "This is my body" may well carry this association, but it is certainly not explicit. So the editors of the new missal sought to emphasize the sacrificial aspect of the Mass at the precise place where it was emphasized classically—at the words over the bread. So on this one I'd say that the new missal in fact does a better job of linking Jesus' words at the Last Supper with our appreciation of the Mass as sacrifice.

In addition, in the present eucharistic prayers there are several explicit references to offering the eucharistic sacrifice. Among these are the classic words of the Roman canon, "We offer to you, God of glory and majesty, this holy and perfect sacrifice, the bread of life and the cup of eternal salvation." Also, in the fourth eucharistic prayer we pray: "Lord, look upon this sacrifice which you have given to your church; and by your Holy Spirit gather all who share this one bread and one cup into the one body of Christ, a living sacrifice of praise." This latter example is particularly poignant and important because it reminds us that we ourselves are to become spiritual sacrifices in the sense that we offer ourselves in service to others (Rom 12:1 ff.). Again, what we find here is ample evidence that what we do at the liturgy should be reflected in the way we live our lives. What Christ did once for all was to offer himself as saving sacrifice for our salvation. What remains to be seen is how well we in fact sacrifice ourselves for the sake of others.

I have one last comment about the structure of the Mass, and this goes back to the rites at the preparation of the gifts. The first proposal for the new Mass eliminated all the prayers said over the bread and wine and the invitation, "Pray brethren" with the response, "May the Lord accept...." Now one of the reasons given why this invitation and response was put back into the missal and remains part of the Mass is precisely because some who evaluated the new Mass thought that the sacrificial elements had been eclipsed too much. The reinsertion of the texts "that our sacrifice will be acceptable" and "may the Lord accept the sacrifice" was one way that the critics of the new missal were to be assuaged. In short, I'd say that there is ample textual and ritual evidence that reflects our belief that the Mass is a sacrifice. But there is also ample evidence to reflect the nature of the Mass as sacrament, meal and table fellowship with other believers in *communion,* that is union with God and with each other in Christ.

VII.

Communion Rite

67. I can understand that the Our Father has a special place in our liturgy, but why has its introduction changed from that of the former Mass to the options the priest can now choose?

Let me begin by underscoring your assertion about the place of the Lord's Prayer at Mass (and at other liturgies revised since Vatican II). This prayer is often referred to as a perfect introduction to the rite of communion, for what we pray is what we now enact. We address God as Father using the words Christ gave us. We have just completed the eucharistic prayer when we join the priest in offering Christ's paschal mystery and ourselves through, with and in him to God the Father, in the unity (communion) of the church in the Holy Spirit. Now we pray in the words that Jesus gave us. This structure is typical of Jewish prayers: naming, addressing and praising God ("hallowed be thy name"), asking for seven petitions (the number was customary at special Jewish feasts) and ending with a final doxology ("for the kingdom, the power and glory are yours"). In two particularly notable segments of the prayer we ask God to "forgive us our sins as we forgive those who sin against us" and to pray "give us this day our daily bread." Therefore, when prayed as part of the rite of communion at Mass, the Lord's Prayer refers to the act of communion to come. In addition the petition "thy kingdom come" can serve as a helpful reminder that at every Mass the Lord's Prayer looks to all future Masses as the fulfillment and completion of the kingdom in eternity. So even as we look to partaking in broken bread and wine poured out, at this point in the Mass we also yearn for the fulfillment of this Mass and of all human life by seeking fulfillment and completion in the kingdom of heaven.

This prayer has also had a distinct role in various rites and rituals, among them the Liturgy of the Hours, and the rite of penance. Because it has classically been understood as the model Christian prayer, the Lord's Prayer has been restored as the conclusion to the intercessions at morning and evening prayer. It has also been restored to a place of emphasis and importance in the rite of communal penance. We pray this prayer together as we are about to confess our sins and receive absolution. Again, the key term here is *forgiveness* from God as well as for and from each other. This same holds true for its place as a part of the rite of communion.

115

Now, about its introduction. Classically, in the Roman rite and in the present Latin edition of the missal, the same invitation is found: "Taught by our Savior's command and formed by the word of God we dare to say...." The sense of this invitation is that we acknowledge that we are really unworthy of what we are engaged in, especially as we pray the words of Jesus and partake in this sacred meal, but that it is only through God's grace that we "dare" *(audemus)* to say these words. Now, what about the present English versions? First, it should be admitted than none of the four options in the present missal carry the association of humility, hesitancy or that we "dare" to speak these words. In fact, the first invitation completely changes the meaning to read, "with confidence"! I'd argue that a more faithful translation retaining some of the humility evident in the Latin would be desirable.

But what about the four invitations in the English missal? Well, in the Appendix to the General Instruction of the Roman Missal for the Dioceses of the USA, the American bishops cite a "circular letter" from Rome's Congregation for Divine Worship of April 27, 1973, dealing with so-called "words of introduction" found throughout the Mass. This official letter indicates that at several places in the Mass what the Latin (or translated) text says may be adapted by the priest to suit particular occasions, distinctive kinds of congregations or varying pastoral needs. One of these invitations is "Before the Lord's Prayer." The letter states that "...by their very nature these brief admonitions do not require that everyone use them in the form in which they appear in the missal." The quote ends with a reminder that such admonitions are to be short and are not to be extended into a mini-homily. ("Less is more.") Therefore, what we have in the present missal are four proposed options with which to introduce the Our Father. Each has a special emphasis and can be used "as is" or as a model. The first, which directs us to approach this prayer "with confidence," makes a statement, albeit different from "we dare to say." The second invitation asserts that we are now to call on God as Father at Jesus' invitation, so "we have the courage to say...." The third is a most poignant text because it emphasizes the theme of forgiveness, so pivotal in this prayer and central to this part of the Mass. The final option is a helpful eschatological text reminding us that all our prayer and work, even this Mass, seeks its fulfillment in the kingdom: "...let us pray for the coming of the kingdom...."

68. In my parish we hold hands during the Our Father, but lately I have heard that this is a problem. Can you explain?

In answering the question (number 65) about postures during the eucharistic prayer, I mentioned in passing the value of appreciating how our bodies are used in worship and that gestures, movement, postures and processions are all part and parcel of worship, specifically the Mass. I would also say that overall we simply haven't "got that right," or at least as right as we could or might get it. In fact, I'd go so far as to argue that overall in the implementation of the reformed liturgy in America, I think we have done fairly well in implementing what takes place at the altar ("in the sanctuary" as we used to say) and that ministers are fairly well trained for the word and the Eucharist. What leaves a lot to be desired is the full bodily involvement in the action of the Mass by the congregation, specifically in the introductory rites, at the presentation of gifts and during the rites of communion. Overall, I would want to urge that we evaluate the quality of our liturgical participation not only by words and the gestures of the ministers but also by how the whole assembly involves itself through postures, symbolic actions and movement as well as words.

Now to your precise question. Let me go back again to the response to question 65, where I spoke about the ancient Christian custom of praying in the standing posture with arms raised and palms open to the heavens. This is called the *orans* position from the Latin for the "praying" posture. Now one of the traditional places during Mass when the whole assembly did assume the *orans* position was during the praying of the Lord's Prayer. This gesture then led to the community's exchanging the sign of peace—another extremely important ritual gesture. Now given the tradition behind the *orans* position as an appropriate posture for the Lord's Prayer and the value that the liturgy has traditionally placed on gestures, I would urge that this be a gesture that the whole assembly would adopt when and where appropriate. Certainly the Lord's Prayer is one such occasion.

However, what happened at the reform of the Mass after Vatican II was that some American parishes adopted the gesture of holding hands during the Lord's Prayer. This obviously signified solidarity and reflected how the rites of communion concerned our relationship with each other as well as our relationship with God through Christ in the act of taking communion. But let's examine the gestures of the rites of communion as a whole and take a look at the text of the Lord's Prayer itself. Clearly, what we have here is a series of gestures that should reflect our speaking to God and our communicating with each other. While the text of the Lord's Prayer refers both to God and to each other ("as we forgive those who trespass against us") we must admit that it primarily concerns what we ask of God through Christ, in seven petitions, after we have named God as Father and invoked praise by saying "hallowed be thy name." For this reason alone some commentators have observed that we might want to revisit the practice of holding hands in favor of reintroducing the *orans* position here. (In fact, the same argument could be made for reintroducing the *orans* position for the whole assembly during the eucharistic prayer while they are standing.) If the assembly were to assume the *orans* position at the Lord's Prayer and then exchange the sign of peace the result would be a balance of bodily involvement—referring both to God and to one another. The last thing I want to do is diminish the assembly's liturgical participation through gestures and postures. I would, however, like to call for a midcourse correction that might make our bodily involvement more appropriate and reflect a theology through gesture that refers both to God and to one another.

69. Why don't we say "for the kingdom, the power and the glory are yours" right after the Our Father? Wouldn't it be more correct, at least ecumenically?

Thank you for making the connection (which not everyone makes) between the phrase "for the kingdom, the power and the glory are yours…" in the present Catholic missal and the more common translation used by other Christian churches: "for thine is the kingdom, and the power, and the glory forever…." Both of these texts serve as "doxologies" to conclude the Lord's Prayer. Some scripture commentators have suggested that this would have been the logical conclusion of a prayer such as the Our Father, just as our eucharistic prayers end with the doxology "through him…all glory and honor is yours almighty Father, forever and ever. Amen." The structure here would follow Jewish liturgical prayers where petitions would be set within a prayer that began and ended with explicit praise of God. Now with regard to these doxologies as you indicate, there are ecumenical implications here that might be better served if we all said the same thing at the same time. Historically, what caused the difference had to do with the translation of the New Testament from its original Greek into other languages, specifically German and Latin. At the time of the

Reformation, Martin Luther undertook the herculean task of translating the Greek New Testament into German, and what he did was to add this doxology as the conclusion of the Lord's Prayer. However, when St. Jerome translated the Greek New Testament into Latin (what we call the Vulgate translation), he did not include this doxology to end the Lord's Prayer. From the time of St. Jerome on, Catholics translated the scriptures from the Vulgate, so it was not surprising that this doxology was not included in such translations or in the Latin Mass texts. (At the risk of oversimplification, we might say that what was thought to be a Protestant-Catholic split was really a matter of whose scripture translation you used. If you used Jerome's, there was no doxology. If you used Luther's, there was a doxology. It took a thousand years for this to become an ecumenical issue!)

Now to answer your question! First, while the American bishops have adopted a number of suggestions put forth for common texts in the Eucharist for the Christian churches, they have not adopted the "ecumenical" translation of the Lord's Prayer. Why? Certainly it is not to diminish the value of prayers that the Christian churches have in common. It is really a pastoral judgment. The fact that people know this prayer by heart and have been taught the present phrasing in the missal led the bishops to judge it best to keep it as it was.

Now with regard to the seeming dislocation of the doxology in the Catholic Mass, as opposed to saying it immediately at the end of the Lord's Prayer, let me offer a bit of liturgical history and precedent from the evolution of the Roman rite. After the final words of the Lord's Prayer in the Roman rite, "but deliver us from evil," it was customary for the priest or bishop to elaborate on this phrase by a text (first of his own composing) that came to be called the embolism to the Our Father. This embolism drew out one or another theme from the previous phrase in light of the feast or season, or in light of the fact that we are about to exchange the sign of peace. Therefore, what gradually emerged in the Roman rite was the establishment of a rather fixed embolism that we now hear in the revised Mass. Note that its first words pick up on the previous words of the Our Father. That is, "deliver us from evil" leads to "deliver us Lord from every evil." The petition to "grant us peace in our day" is a subtle introduction to the sign of peace to follow. The time frame, "as we wait in joyful hope for the coming of our Savior Jesus Christ," is particularly significant, as once again it underscores the eschatological ("not yet") character of all worship (and the whole Christian life). We await Christ's return in glory at the end of time to bring the temporal world to an end (recall the acclamation "Lord Jesus, come in glory"). How fitting, therefore, that the doxology itself should end with coupling "now and forever."

Despite these differences of exactly where the doxology occurs, I think it must be admitted that its insertion into the missal so everyone can hear the embolism is significant, and the addition of the doxology for all to pray is also a significant, if small, step toward ecumenical unity. Also, the fact that the embolism has found a place in the Roman rite since the early centuries and is part of our Catholic tradition makes me want to at least name this as a "Catholic" value and practice whose theology is significant: peace, eschatology and doxology all in one!

70. Is the priest supposed to invite us to exchange the sign of peace at every Mass? Should he come down to the congregation to exchange it with us?

Among the reforms of the Mass after Vatican II, the restoration of the sign of peace was one that drew a lot of attention and some heated debate! One obvious reason was that it asked congregations to engage other persons around them at the very time when they customarily would be praying silently before receiving communion (as they watched the priest receive communion). The sign of peace, despite its name, caused no little upheaval!

Historically, we know that the whole assembly joined in exchanging the sign of peace as a ritual gesture signifying unity, reconciliation and a deepening share in Christ's peace. However, just as many of the ritual gestures that "belonged" to the people came to be engaged in by the priest and other ministers only, so too, the sign of peace was a clerical preserve at the solemn high Tridentine Mass. According to the rubrics for the Tridentine Mass, after the breaking of the bread and the lamb of God acclamations, the priest would say the prayer that we now have: "Lord Jesus Christ, you said to your apostles I leave you peace, my peace I give to you...." Then if the sign of peace was offered, he would kiss the altar (the symbol of Christ himself) and give the peace to the deacon, who gave it in turn to the subdeacon, who in turn would exchange it with other ministers and eventually the people in a chain-like procedure.

The new missal rearranged part of the communion rite so that after the doxology, "for the kingdom, the power and the glory are yours...," the priest says the "Lord Jesus Christ" prayer, addressing the entire assembly with the text, "the peace of the Lord be with you always," followed by the exchange of the sign of peace. Now this is where the answer to your precise question lies. In the missal it states that the priest or deacon *may add* "let us offer each other the sign of peace." So to the first part of your question the missal says that the priest/deacon "may" invite the assembly to exchange the sign of peace. However, given our liturgical history it would seem most appropriate to exchange it on a regular basis and therefore (at least mentally) to change "may" to "normally adds." This ritual gesture can signify our relatedness in Christ and to each other, which has been solidified in the celebration of Mass itself.

Other interesting changes in this rite from that of the Tridentine Mass include the fact that the priest no longer kisses the altar and that the people exchange the sign of peace among themselves. The rationale here is that the assembly of believers is itself a sign of the presence of Christ and hence the body of Christ can and should share the peace of Christ with one another without having to wait for the peace to "come from the sanctuary." Now with regard to the nature of the gesture to be used, the missal states that this is done "according to local custom." In most parishes I'd say that the handshake is the most common gesture. For some, an embrace might be a better gesture. For families, even a kiss might be most appropriate. If the handclasp is used, one suggestion from the (American) Bishops' Committee on the Liturgy statement, *The Sign of Peace* (1977), is that we might consider using two hands to shake the hands of our neighbor. This would signify a deeper commitment to the other than the handclasp that is common in ordinary business and social life. After all, what we wish is that the peace of *Christ* might take deeper root and be a source of reconciliation and accomplish in us a fuller experience of God's favor and grace.

As to whether the priest should come down to the congregation, there is frankly no fixed rule. The missal states that the priest "gives the sign of peace to the deacon or minister." In the document *The Sign of Peace* the value of having the people exchange this gesture with each other is upheld, with the caution that if the clergy try to "reach out and touch" everyone, or even the majority of the assembly, then this could come across as heavily weighted in favor of a clerical imposition. On the other hand, the same statement suggests that if the priest avoids any contact with persons other than the ministers, then this could be perceived to be a sign of clericalism. The document suggests, therefore, that the priest should exchange it with some members of the congregation. It is hard for me to try to establish a rule of thumb here because of the many variations among churches and worship spaces. I would generally tend to want to exchange the peace with some of the liturgical ministers and some of the people in the first row of chairs or pews.

71. When should the sign of peace be observed—in its present place, at the penitential rite or at the presentation of the gifts?

In the earliest evidence we have of the Roman liturgy (Justin the Martyr and Hippolytus, for example), the sign of peace was exchanged at the time of the presentation of the gifts. Then, by the fourth century it was changed to its present location. It was never performed at the penitential rite. Let me try to explain why it was where it has been and why it would not be in the introductory rites of the Mass.

The principal reason why the sign of peace was first exchanged after the Liturgy of the Word and before the gifts were presented was to conform with Jesus' teaching in the gospel of Matthew (5:23–24): "If you bring your gift to the altar and there recall that your brother has anything against you, leave your gift at the altar, go first to be reconciled with your brother, and then come and offer your gift." Not surprisingly, purity of intention should match the giving of the gift, and a deep integration of what is celebrated and what is lived makes the offering of worship the more desirable. The fact that this point was the location for the practice in the West and remains the location for the sign of peace in many Eastern rites is the reason why the theology of the proclaimed word is often cited as the basis for our reconciliation. What God offers us through the proclaimed word—the good news of salvation in Christ—is to be offered to each other in worship and in life. What God "creates" through the proclaimed and preached word is the "becoming" of reality in human life.

In the West, by the fourth century, however, the exchanging of the peace sign shifted to its present location. Among others, St. Augustine offers another theological explanation as to why it is located after the Lord's Prayer and before communion. In one of his sermons (number

227), he indicates that the gesture of the sign of peace requires that worshipers demonstrate through this sign what they have just prayed: "...forgive us...as we forgive." He also indicates that it is appropriate that after we have exchanged the sign of peace, we then approach sacramental communion and receive the Body of Christ, which term for Augustine refers both to taking the eucharistic species in communion and to the church as Christ's body (from the poignant metaphor of St. Paul in 1 Corinthians). Hence, the present location can be considered traditional from the fourth century on in the Roman rite, and the gesture itself should be understood in relation to the praying of the Our Father and the reception of communion.

On the basis of these strong liturgical precedents and the theological reasoning behind them, I'd be hard pressed to think that the sign of peace should be exchanged at the penitential rite. What we now call the penitential rite originated as the priest's private prayers of devotion, recited in the sacristy before the Eucharist began. Hence the weight we should give to it is minor compared with the proclamation of the Word and the eucharistic action itself. Now what does occur on some occasions is that before Mass begins a commentator will address the assembly and invite them to greet each other. This is done with a view toward what the introductory rites are to accomplish—namely "that the faithful coming together take on the form of a community..." (General Instruction, n. 24; for more on this, see the section above on introductory rites). This kind of greeting could enhance the sense of belonging to a community when the congregation that comes together is disparate and have gathered for a particular occasion, for example, the celebration of a marriage, ordination, baptism or confirmation.

Over the years since the reform of the missal following Vatican II, there have been several discussions in official church circles (specifically in the United States Bishops' Conference and in Rome) about the possibility of allowing the priest to choose which of these classical places to locate the sign of peace at a particular Mass. Some suggest that this option would be most useful to help emphasize elements of one liturgical season over another. For example, since Lent is traditionally an important time to reflect on God's Word and come to deeper conversion through obeying it, the option of exchanging the sign of peace after the proclamation of the Word would be a good way to ratify what we have enacted in the announcement of the Word. Alternatively, the present location for the peace sign would subtly underscore how the Eucharist is considered *the* sacrament of the Easter season. (The background here is that after his resurrection Jesus appeared to the disciples at meals, for example, either at the shore or at table on the way to Emmaus.) This meal fellowship received a sacramental dimension for us because the fifty days of the Easter season was the first season we can document when the Eucharist was celebrated daily. This custom led to the summary phrase that Easter was fifty days of the "paschal communion" in the risen Christ. Therefore, to exchange the sign of peace before receiving communion would be a gestural way of articulating what Augustine has so carefully argued: that our share in the Eucharist is a sign of our sharing life with each other in the body of Christ.

72. Why does the priest mingle a small piece of the consecrated host into the cup? What is its significance?

It may come as a surprise at first but the principal reason why part of the consecrated bread is dropped into the chalice has to do with church unity! Let me give some theological background and historical precedents for it.

Every act of liturgy is done for the sake of those present and for the church throughout the world. That's why, for example, the general intercessions always exhort us to pray for the concerns of the whole church and the wider world. Another way that this universal dimension of the Mass is underscored is by the inclusion of prayers for the unity and peace of the church (often in prayers over the gifts and prayers after communion). Another way that the liturgy signifies the universality of what we celebrate is through what was originally called the rite of the *fermentum* (meaning a particle of consecrated bread). Pope Innocent I in the fifth century wrote that because of the large numbers of Christians in Rome they all could not gather together for the pope's Eucharist on a given Sunday. Hence the pope would send acolytes from the papal Sunday Mass with parts of the eucharistic bread that he had consecrated. The pastors of Rome's parish churches would place this eucharistic bread in the chalice at the Masses they were celebrating as a sign of unity and communion with the pope's Eucharist and with all of the Masses celebrated in the city. So this seemingly insignificant gesture symbolically confirmed the concept of church unity, solidarity with the pope, and the theological rationale supporting the observance of Sunday as *the* day to gather for Mass. Distance, however, prevented the *fermentum* from being sent to the rural parishes.

Many other parishes of the Christian world began to adopt another custom that somewhat replicated this rite. This was called the *sancta*, and it more closely resembles what you see at Mass now, but not exactly. What began to happen was that priests, on their own, would take a particle of the consecrated bread and place it on the altar at the time of the breaking of the bread. It would remain there until the next Mass that was celebrated at that altar. At that time, the priest would drop this particle of bread into the chalice and alternatively leave a fragment for the next Mass, and so forth. The theology of church unity is reflected in this rite, but also it emphasizes how one Mass leads to the next Mass, until the kingdom comes. The principal theological reason is that the Mass is never solely for those who gather for it, as though it were a closed club. The Mass is always for believers in the whole church, and at every Mass those who gather intercede for the church throughout the world and for the needs of the whole world.

73. Some priests change the words that invite us to receive communion. Can you explain?

According to the missal, at the "invitation to communion" the priest says, "Happy are those who are called to his supper." Sometimes you might hear the words, "Happy are we who are called to this supper/table," or other variations. What I'd like to suggest as I try to explain the difference is that many of the texts we use in the liturgy have more than one meaning, even though one meaning might be more apparent than another. The principle here is called *multivalence*. If you have any familiarity with chemistry (and here my high school chemistry teacher would either cringe about what I'm going to say or be proud that I at least did remember this!) you will recall that part of it was based on the periodic chart of *valences*, a word that signifies "meaning" or "meanings." When you add the prefix *multi* (from the Latin *multis*) meaning "many," then this term is a shorthand way of saying that sometimes the words we use at Mass have many meanings. The priest's statement just before communion is one such text with many meanings.

The text at this point in the missal ("happy are those called to his supper") is taken from the Book of Revelation (19:9) prefiguring the end of time, when the elect are called to eternal union with God. The imagery used here is that of being called to the wedding feast in the kingdom of heaven. The priest's words here are not only a call to communion but a reminder of our invitation to the banquet of the lamb in the kingdom of heaven. Therefore, when the missal uses the pronoun "they" it quotes Revelation and refers to all those who one day will experience eternal life. Again, the technical term used to describe this kind of statement is "eschatological." Essentially, this kind of prayer is a reminder that our ultimate goal is eternal life in heaven. The precise metaphor for it in the Book of Revelation is that we hope to join all those who are called to "the supper of the Lamb." It signifies that what we do at Mass is meant to lead to its final consummation at the eternal banquet with God in heaven.

Now in the present Roman rite, we have very few such references to this "eschatological" aspect of the Eucharist. Probably the major reason is that our Roman Catholic theology of eucharistic sacrifice and offering and the intercessory power of the Mass grew in importance over the centuries in light of the debates stemming from the Reformation. Therefore, it is not surprising that our present missal should continue to emphasize the power of what we do here and now. But there is always a dimension of the Mass that signifies that we are not there yet and that the Eucharist is a kind of promise of what we shall experience in its fullness in the kingdom of heaven.

When the priest changes words such as "they" to "we" and "his supper" to "this supper," he is inviting us to take communion at this Mass. But that is really only part of what this text means. It also means that what we share here and now will lead us to a sharing in the eternal, heavenly banquet in eternity. Strictly speaking, therefore, there is great merit to keeping the text as it is so that its many meanings about coming to this communion *and* the eternal banquet can be conveyed by the single phrase from the Book of Revelation.

But for the sake of completion and nuance, I need to point out that in some of the Eastern rites the invitation text contains the phrase, "Holy things for the holy." This suggests that what we take in communion is to make us, the baptized people of God, God's "holy ones," even holier through this act of eucharistic communion. I'd also say that this is quite legitimate because at this part of the Mass we are invited to communion. But the reason why I'd like to keep the clear eschatological phrasing in our present missal is that, unlike the Eastern rites, we refer to this "not yet" aspect of the Eucharist in very few places. The Eastern rites, however, have strong emphases in this direction in the texts and rites of their liturgy of the Mass. On this point, I think we in the West can learn an important lesson from the East.

74. Why do some people kneel on one knee before receiving communion?

There are a number of issues at stake here when you describe the gesture of kneeling on one knee and the proper manner of receiving communion. Let me begin by making a distinction between kneeling and genuflecting. Normally, the word "kneeling" connotes remaining for some time on one's knees (usually both). This was the most common gesture assumed by the congregation during the Tridentine Mass. "Genuflecting," however, refers to touching the floor with one knee and assuming the standing position immediately thereafter. I suspect that you are referring to the genuflection that some people perform just prior to receiving communion. I say "some people" because, as you suggest in your question, this has not been stipulated as a gesture that all must perform.

In at least three places in the General Instruction of the Roman Missal in descriptions of how the congregation receives communion, we find the phrase, "…the communicants approach, make the proper reverence, and stand in front of the priest…" to receive communion (see nn. 244, 246, 247). These citations were reiterated in the 1980 document, The Inestimable Gift, which the Eucharist is for the church (the Latin title is *Inaestimabile donum*). In this document certain abuses or deviations from required church practice regarding the Eucharist were explained and clarified. One example concerned the manner of receiving communion (n. 11), and this document reiterated that the General Instruction specified that a proper sign of reverence should be given to the eucharistic species. What's at the heart of your precise question is what does "make the proper reverence" mean?

First of all, this gesture should be understood in relation to all the other symbolic gestures of the Mass, such as kissing the altar and the gospel book, bowing before the altar at the beginning and end of Mass, making the sign of the cross at the beginning and end of Mass and so forth. Given the fact that the Mass contains a veritable ensemble of signs, symbols and gestures, it is logical that as we approach to receive communion we make a sign of reverence to the eucharistic species itself. What the missal specifies is that the communicant stands to receive communion. But the question of what the sign of reverence before reception should be is left open. I suspect that because the priest genuflects before inviting the assembly to communion that some people would want to choose this as a sign of reverence. On the other hand, some people come forward in procession and bow before the consecrated bread and wine. Others may make a sign of the cross on their forehead or lips. This variety is quite legitimate. The liturgical issue here is that we engage our bodies in showing a sign of respect as we approach to receive the Eucharist.

75. Is it more reverent to receive communion on the tongue?

Let me begin by recalling what I said in response to question 65 (regarding the postures for the eucharistic prayer). A major goal of liturgy is to provide a structure for the appropriate use of our bodies to express what we say and do at Mass. Then, in response to the previous question, I cited the directives about the customary reverence to be given through our bodies to what we are doing at this part of the Mass. Now, you ask a more precise question about what is the better way to receive communion—on the tongue or in the hand. In summarizing some liturgical history in this response, I'd like to combine the evidence of what people *did* to show their reverence to the Eucharist with what they understood the Eucharist to be. This may help explain where we have come from and the rationale for having two options for the way we can receive communion today.

One of the main sources for explanations about the rites of the Mass and their theological meanings from the fourth and fifth centuries are documents called mystagogic catecheses. Now that first word "mystagogic" has recently returned to our church vocabulary by way of the Rite for the Christian Initiation of Adults. After adults have received sacramental initiation they now experience a period of "unpacking" what happened to them in what is called the period of mystagogy. This term is taken from the Greek and means to be instructed in the mysteries. (Recall here that "mysteries" does not mean what is unknown, but what is so profound and significant that it cannot but be described as the sacred mysteries of Christ's love poured out for us, which we experience through the rites of the liturgy.) Now the origin of this period of continuing formation was the fourth century, when bishops would instruct the newly initiated about what happened to them at the Easter vigil. One example of these mystagogic catecheses is from St. Cyril, ordained bishop in Jerusalem in the fourth century (actually about 351). During Lent he met frequently with those to be baptized and instructed them in the faith (these are called catecheses or catechetical lectures). He then met with them every day during the week after Easter to explain the meaning of the sacred mysteries of initiation. The last two of them concern the Eucharist. The first of these explains how the Eucharist is food for immortality; the second describes the meaning of what occurs in the rites and gestures of the Mass. For Cyril, the dominant image was that the Eucharist was a sacred *meal* and what the faithful and the newly initiated received was *food* for the journey of life. In the second of these catecheses on how to receive communion, Cyril explains that it be received in the hand precisely because, as food, we take it as we take other foods. Then he tells them that when they approach to receive from now on they are to make their left hand a kind of throne for their right hand so that they can receive the eucharistic bread in the palm of their right hand and say "Amen" as they receive it. After they consume the bread they are to approach to receive the eucharistic cup and say "Amen" to what they receive, the "cup of his Blood."

This combination of directives on how to receive communion reflected the predominant image at the time that the Eucharist was the meal for the pilgrim church's journey to the kingdom of heaven. In Cyril's theology the eucharistic action was the central *image* and *foretaste* of the fullness of experiencing the risen Lord, which will occur only in the eternal kingdom of heaven. Hence, he understands that the Eucharist is central but provisional, a fully real but promissory presence of the whole exalted Christ in eternity.

By the ninth century, the context of explaining what the Eucharist was and how to receive it changed. Part of this had to do with the way people now could comprehend what was real and what was not. Succinctly put, the agenda now was to explain what the eucharistic species itself was. The focus was no longer on explaining what the whole rite (gathering, word, eucharistic prayer, communion, dismissal) meant theologically and spiritually. From the ninth century on, there was a shift to an emphasis on what the eucharistic species was and an increased reverence for the species as the place of the real presence of Christ himself. This was also the time when the church came to emphasize the moment of consecration at the words, "This is my body...blood." It is not a surprise, therefore, that at this time theologians and bishops would emphasize the uniqueness of Christ's presence in bread and wine; when the laity did receive communion (which became more and more infrequent) they were not to touch the species itself but should extend their tongues as an act of reverence.

Before we choose one period over another, it should be recalled here that both periods and examples emphasized the theology of the Eucharist as food sustaining us as the pilgrim church. The food that Cyril described so profoundly, in the Middle Ages came to be appreciated as one of the medicines that we need to help heal and cure us as we journey to the kingdom of heaven. What also occurs is a clear shift of emphasis to the act of consecration and the (rare) act of receiving communion. The customary gesture during the eucharistic prayer was kneeling; the customary way to receive was on the tongue.

What has occurred after the Vatican II reform of the Mass has been an appropriate reemphasis on the Eucharist as food and on the eucharistic prayer as our solemn proclamation of "thanks and praise," which we now hear prayed aloud and in which we participate by acclamations. These emphases in the rite have led many conferences of bishops to request that people be allowed to have the option of receiving communion in the hand, which gesture would ratify these renewed emphases in the liturgy of the Mass and in the theology of the Eucharist today.

Although I took the long way, the answer to your question is that either gesture may be chosen today and that the return of the opportunity to receive in the hand demonstrates a renewed appreciation of the Eucharist as the food of immortality. However, whatever manner of receiving communion is chosen, the way we receive should be marked with signs of reverence and devotion. There should be nothing casual about receiving the Eucharist. Therefore, we can profit from thinking about how well we extend the palm of our hands to the eucharistic minister, how reverently we take the Eucharist and with what conviction and commitment we say "Amen" to the declaration, "Body of Christ."

76. I seem to remember that in the Tridentine Mass the priest said a much longer prayer when I received communion than the phrase, "Body/Blood of Christ," and our response, "Amen." Can you explain?

You are quite right that the prayer the priest used to say when distributing communion was longer and did not require a response. (What may be of interest here is that when I checked the Latin edition of the Tridentine missal used by the priest at the altar I found no directions about the manner of distributing communion! But in one of the pre–Vatican II hand missals used by the faithful, I did find the directives for distribution. But even here, what is notable is that there is a red line across the page at the beginning and end of this section. Might one legitimately conjecture that the directives for the former Mass concerned only what the priest did and that communion distribution was considered at the very least "something else"?)

What is clear is that, based on the former missal, before he received communion, the priest said to himself, "May the body of our Lord Jesus Christ preserve my soul for everlasting life, Amen." He then changed the text slightly as he drank from the chalice: "May the blood...." Now when he distributed communion (under the species of the bread only), he said this same prayer as he gave each communicant the host on the tongue; he simply changed the pronoun to say (in Latin) "...preserve your soul...." The only bit of personal recollection I can add to this was that as an altar server who held the paten under the chin of those receiving communion, I noticed that the priest did not always say this whole text for each communicant. I suspect that as people started to receive communion more and more frequently and regularly and as their numbers grew, priests judged that communion would take too much time if they said this prayer over each person receiving.

The present instruction in the missal, that the minister say "Body of Christ" and the communicant respond "Amen," returns to a practice that is amply documented in the patristic era, specifically by St. Augustine. The new *Catechism of the Catholic Church* cites his text in full (n. 1396) from one of his sermons (no. 272) in which he describes what occurs at communion. He emphasizes who we are who come to receive: members of Christ. Hence, what we receive is really who we are—the Body of Christ. Therefore, he exhorts us to say "Amen" ("yes, it is true") to the Eucharist and to live as a member of the body of Christ. What we have here is another example of what I have referred to before as the *multivalence* (many meanings) of liturgical texts. One meaning concerns our assent in faith to the Eucharist as Christ's Body; but another level concerns our assent to living with each other as members of Christ's Body. Based on what we have been saying throughout much of this book, what we have here is not surprising—namely an emphasis on the church, the community with whom we celebrate Mass, and not just on the eucharistic species. Recalling the actual text of the Tridentine rite, you will notice that it emphasized individual salvation ("preserve my/your soul"). The return in the new missal to "Body of Christ" requires not only a verbal response "Amen," but a commitment to living with each other as members of Christ.

77. Why is it that sometimes only the priest and those at the altar receive from the chalice? Why not the whole congregation? Are there regulations that govern when the laity can receive from the chalice?

If you experience a Mass in which only the priest and those at the altar receive from the chalice, this is either because of custom or because a particular bishop has prohibited the distribution under both species on Sundays. But perhaps I'm getting ahead of myself. Once more, a little historical background and a review of current teaching can help here.

Certainly it has always been the custom that the priest received both the eucharistic bread and cup. Up through the twelfth century, the laity who received at all also customarily communicated from the chalice. As I have already noted when discussing the piety and practices about the Eucharist in the Middle Ages, certain shifts occurred, not the least of which involved the withholding of the chalice from the laity. Theologically, the doctrine that was part of the reason that laity received less and less from the chalice was the doctrine of *concomitance*. This teaching (officially ratified by the church's magisterium in 1551 at the Council of Trent) was that Christ was totally present in either the eucharistic bread or the eucharistic wine. Hence, if one received one of the species, one received the whole, sacramental Christ.

The present General Instruction of the Roman Missal marks a dramatic shift away from the practice of restricting the chalice, but it does not teach anything at variance with the doctrine of concomitance. It states that communion "has a more complete form as a sign when it is received under both kinds" (n. 240). It goes on to stress that when it is so received it better images the notion of the Eucharist as a banquet and it indicates that this image of banquet is the better preparation for the "eschatological banquet in the Father's kingdom," which our present Eucharist anticipates and prepares for. The *sign* value described here is important. It recalls that Jesus' invitation at the Last Supper was *both* to take and eat as well as to take and drink. This same General Instruction listed over a dozen occasions when communion under two species could be offered to the whole assembly. In 1970 the bishops of the United States added another five or so occasions, the most significant being that this permission was extended to weekdays. Then in 1978 the American bishops voted to extend this permission to Sundays with the approval of the diocesan bishop. In the intervening years I have been in only two dioceses in this country where the bishops have not permitted the distribution of the chalice to the laity. Yet I have been in some parishes where the custom has been not to offer the chalice to all the faithful.

Sometimes I find that we need to examine what we do by force of (bad) habit and revisit decisions made some time ago. Certainly, the official line of argumentation from the General Instruction of the Roman Missal through the directives of the United States bishops has been in the direction of extending this permission and practice.

78. What does the church teach regarding the practice of intinction. Is it forbidden?

First of all, so that all of us can be clear, *intinction* refers to the practice of offering the laity a share in the eucharistic species by dipping the consecrated bread into consecrated wine. This was first documented in the West in seventh-century Spain and is found in descriptions of the Mass through the era when the faithful no longer received under two species. In the East, this has been a common practice since about the ninth century. When communion is distributed in this way in Eastern rites, the eucharistic bread is leavened, with a cubelike shape, and pieces are placed in the chalice for the priest to distribute to the faithful by a spoon.

As a means of communicating under two species, this practice was restored to the Western (Roman) church in 1965. It is still included in the General Instruction of the Roman Missal as one way to distribute communion (see nn. 246–47). In practice, however, if communion is offered under two species, it is commonly done by having everyone drink directly from the chalice (see General Instruction, nn. 244–45). There are several reasons for this, but they derive principally from the way the General Instruction describes the *sign* value of communion under both forms. Jesus said "Take and eat…take and drink." Hence, this admonition sanctions two parallel actions for sharing in the consecrated bread and wine—just as we take food and drink in parallel actions at mealtimes in daily life. The custom of dunking is very limited in our culture; some would suggest that it is not proper etiquette at all!

Furthermore, in pastoral practice if intinction is *the* option for receiving communion, then we take away a person's legitimate right not to receive under both forms. This is especially problematic when recovering alcoholics want to receive communion, and the option of one species is not offered to them. In addition, given the longstanding custom in the West that we use unleavened bread for the Eucharist, the use of wafer-thin bread makes it difficult to dip it into the chalice and distribute on the tongue. Issues of personal hygiene (saliva and so forth) come into play here in what can be characterized as providing at least potentially awkward circumstances and results.

For me, the issue of eucharistic symbolism and sign value come into play very significantly. By this I mean that the genre of the Eucharist is a meal and that whatever we can do to restore this "feeling" to our experience of the Mass the better. (Of course, this is also to assert that it is a sacred, ritualized meal and a sacrament of the sacrifice of Christ.) At its heart, what the church does in sacraments is to take what we normally do and use in human life and ritualize it for our public worship. Therefore, what we do at human meals—eat, drink, converse and such—is what we do at the Mass. We take bread and wine, bless them and give them to the church for spiritual nourishment and sustenance. The better the sign value of taking, eating and drinking in the Mass itself, the more faithful we are to what the liturgy of the Mass implies and contains. Therefore, I'd say that while intinction is permitted (as is taking the eucharistic wine through a tube or from a spoon, see General Instruction, nn. 248–52), the norm should be the distribution of communion under both forms from the paten and the chalice—for eating *and* drinking.

79. Where do the extra consecrated bread and wine go?

When I reviewed the kinds of church documents I have been citing throughout this book to determine exactly what they say in answer to your question, I was surprised that they do not offer an answer! This is to say that the directions of the missal and its General Instruction do not tell us what to do with the extra consecrated bread and wine. I do not know why this is. But I can use this evidence (or rather lack of it) to make the general comment that liturgical documents concern the act of liturgy itself, and, theologically, this means they are concerned with how to conduct the dynamic event of word and sacrament that we call the Mass. Your question really concerns what happens to the consecrated species when they are not used in the liturgy. In other words, you are asking about what derives from the celebration, not really the celebration itself. Therefore the liturgy documents would not cover your concern.

The answer lies in the custom of the church to reserve the remaining eucharistic bread normally in a tabernacle. This word can be traced to the Latin *tabernaculum,* which means "tent." This term derives from the scriptures, where the notion of God's dwelling in a tent with the chosen people is the basis for the pivotal text in the prologue of the gospel of St. John: "…the Word became flesh and dwelt among us" (Jn 1:14). The verb "dwelt" derives from this term—"tabernacle"—meaning that Jesus "pitched his tent" among us. Customarily, the tabernacle is a square or boxlike vessel with a door and a key with a lock. According to the post–Vatican II norms for church building and architecture, it should be placed in a chapel separate from the main body of the church or the place where the liturgy is celebrated (see *Eucharisticum Mysterium,* n.53). The rationale for this separation is that the action of the Mass leads to the place of reservation and that the fitting act of adoration before the reserved Eucharist in the tabernacle is not the same thing as the variety of actions, postures, words and symbolic gestures that we engage in during the Mass itself. The present norms also state that where the tabernacle cannot be in a separate chapel, it should be in a conspicuous location, one that is suited for personal prayer and adoration.

Some historical perspective can help here. In the early church, the Eucharist was reserved primarily so that the sick, elderly, or others who could not celebrate the Mass with the community would receive communion from the reserved sacrament. Then, because the Eucharist was reserved, it became a legitimate object of adoration and devotion. This historical precedent helps us understand that even modern papal teaching (e.g., Pius XII's *Mediator Dei*) regarding the reserved sacrament states that its primary rationale is for distribution to the sick and that secondarily it becomes a proper object of devotion.

Also, the architectural evidence we have of places for reservation includes a variety of vessels suspended on a wire in the church (one term for such a vessel is "pyx") or that the eucharistic bread was placed in a "sacrament house" or in a sacristy cupboard. That the tabernacle became the most common location and was placed on an altar derives from a sixteenth-century custom, which was eventually legislated in the nineteenth century for all churches.

Certainly, one of the most pastorally effective practices since Vatican II has been the way deacons, acolytes and eucharistic ministers have taken up the practice of bringing communion to the sick after Sunday Mass. Sometimes, such persons are dismissed from the Sunday assembly with the priest's blessing and the prayer of the community. When this is done on weekdays, the Eucharist is taken from the tabernacle.

As for the leftover wine, again we have no instructions in the missal, nor do we have any evidence from architectural guidelines that there is anything parallel to the tabernacle for the leftover consecrated wine. By custom, the leftover wine is consumed after communion or after Mass by the ministers of the liturgy and members of the congregation.

80. Is the priest supposed to bring the consecrated hosts to the tabernacle? Must he clean the chalice at the altar after communion?

Again, as in my answer to the previous question, the lack of data about this in the new missal and its General Instruction means that we rely on custom, since it is informed by the present liturgical directives. I would say that in light of the fact that deacons (as well as priests) are regarded as ordinary ministers of communion and that acolytes and extraordinary ministers help in communion distribution, any of these persons could bring the consecrated bread to the tabernacle. What the missal does say is that, after communion, "the priest may return to the chair" and that "a period of silence may now be observed, or a psalm or song of praise may be sung." What I find important about this directive is that it emphasizes once more the value of periods of silence in the celebration of Mass, and that if the priest returns to the chair (which I would regard as preferable), this would indicate a location separate from the altar where the concluding rites are more properly conducted.

With regard to the cleansing of the eucharistic vessels, the missal contains much information. In the directives for the Mass itself, it states that "the vessels are cleansed by the priest or deacon or acolyte after the communion or after Mass, if possible, at the side table." This text refers to the (longer) description in the General Instruction of the Roman Missal (n. 238), which adds that wine and water or water alone are used to cleanse the chalice; the purificator (white linen cloth) is used to wipe the paten. All of this is done by the one who is purifying the vessels. This marks a dramatic shift from the previous missal, where it stated that only the priest could do this. Another dramatic shift from the previous missal locates the cleansing of the vessels at a side table, not the main altar.

What all of this suggests is that whatever is customary in your church regarding these actions might well need to be reviewed and adjusted in light of what the missal actually says, especially if any proposed adjustment would allow more time for silent prayer after communion.

81. Why are the rites after communion so short?

The short answer is that their purpose is to end the celebration and dismiss the community. In fact the rites after communion are really divided into two parts, one being the prayer after communion and the other what *The Sacramentary* calls the concluding rites. In fact *The Sacramentary* places the prayer after communion as part of the communion rite itself. It follows the distribution and is preceded by a period of silence.

The concluding rites now follow. They consist of "any brief announcements" (General Instruction, n. 123), the priest's greeting ("the Lord be with you" and so forth), the priest's blessing and the deacon's statement of dismissal ("Go in the peace of Christ" and so forth), followed by the priest's kissing the altar and the procession out of the church. Let's take a look at each of these.

First of all, the announcements *follow* the prayer after communion. The reasoning here is that the period of silence after receiving communion should not be interrupted by parish announcements followed by the prayer—I say this because I know of many parishes where this is the custom. I suspect the rationale is that the people are already seated after communion, so why not do the announcements then? The more proper thing is to pray in silence, listen to the priest's prayer and then present the announcements. It is very interesting to note in the documentation we have from the early church, when deacons normally assisted at Mass, that it was the deacon who made the announcements. The reason was that because of his day-to-day ministry, he would know who was sick or in need of the community's charity and what community events were on the calendar. What is seemingly a "housekeeping" task really is meant to carry theological weight—namely, that altar and daily life are intrinsically connected.

The formula for the blessing itself may be as simple as, "May almighty God bless you, the Father, and the Son, and the Holy Spirit." However, one of the features of the present missal is the addition of twenty options for the threefold "solemn blessings" and some twenty-six options for a concluding "prayer over the people" as part of these concluding rites. Since the priest may choose any of these at any time, I would suggest that a solemn blessing might best be used for Sundays of the seasons of Advent, Christmas, Lent and Easter (and *The Sacramentary* provides blessings designed for these seasons) or other solemn or special occasions. On less festive days, the priest might choose a prayer over the people as part of the concluding rites. The only caution I might offer is that we should be attentive to how much of the Mass is spoken texts and that there should be a balance of speaking, singing, silence and listening. To add another spoken prayer to a Mass with a lot of speaking might be to "overload" it and make it heavy with words.

The deacon's dismissal may be from one of three forms in *The Sacramentary*, all of which are derived from the classical dismissal in the Roman rite (*Ite missa est*, which as I noted in answer to question 1, is the origin of the term "Mass"), "The Mass is ended, go in peace." Now what normally follows is a recessional hymn or other music. In fact this is not found in the missal or its Instruction, principally because it is not an intrinsic part of the liturgy itself. What caused this to become a custom for us derives from the rigid strictures of the former Tridentine Mass and the concern that the congregation come to participate actively in the Mass. Beginning in the 1940s in Europe and spreading to this country afterward was a custom whereby the assembly joined in hymns at three or four places in the Mass, which singing added to what was in the Tridentine missal, and which therefore could be sung by the people without prejudicing the obligation of the priest to do all and say all that was in the missal. Therefore, the people would sing a hymn at the entrance, at the offertory, at communion and after the dismissal. That this became a common way for people to participate in at least some parts of the Mass is evident in the way the recessional song retains its importance in the present Mass despite the fact that it is not part of the Mass itself.

82. What is the purpose of the prayer after communion? I seem to recall that sometimes it's about dismissal and other times about the hope of heaven.

Let me begin by recalling that word "multivalence" once again. What I want to suggest here is that we recall the principle that texts and parts of the Mass can have many meanings. What we should do to answer your question is to examine what these texts themselves say, and from this investigation offer a summary insight about the nature of this prayer. I say this especially because the present missal is very reticent about stating what themes this prayer should have. It simply states that "in the prayer after communion, the priest petitions for the effects of the mystery just celebrated..." (n. 56 k). Among other things, sometimes this prayer refers to the hope of heaven (see First Sunday of Advent) or living what we have celebrated (Christmas Mass at Midnight) or experiencing more fully the gift of salvation (Mary, Mother of God, January 1) or our response to the Eucharist by welcoming Christ in others (Baptism of the Lord). If I were asked for a brief explanation of the theme of this prayer, I would say that it most often refers to living out what we have celebrated in daily life and that it underscores how the Eucharist leads us to eternal life with God in the kingdom of heaven.

VIII.

MUSIC AT MASS

83. What kind of music is allowed at Mass?

Your question raises a number of issues, both theoretical and practical. I'd say that no single feature of the revision of the Mass has had as much pastoral impact as has the reintroduction of popular participation at Mass through music. Allow me to offer three observations as I try to answer your important question: what Vatican II says about style, the procedure for implementing the liturgical reforms of Vatican II and some of the governing principles for determining suitable music for Mass (from Vatican II and subsequent liturgical documents).

When discussing sacred art and sacred furnishings in general the Liturgy Constitution states that "the Church has not adopted any particular style of art as its very own but has admitted styles from every period, according to the proper genius and circumstances of peoples and the requirements of the many different rites in the Church" (n. 123). This is a very important text because it respects variety in the styles of art that can and should be used in the liturgy, while at the same time it insists on the value of the use of arts in worship. I have spoken on a few occasions in this book about our using in liturgy things that are native to us as humans in our common worship of God. One of these is our talent to create things of beauty, which act of creation reflects the beauty, truth and goodness of the living God. Our gifts for ingenuity and artistic creativity are always brought to bear in the act of worship. But over the course of the centuries these gifts have been used in varied and different ways, depending, among other things, on the needs of the liturgy at the time and the culture of the time. It is for this reason primarily that this same Liturgy Constitution insists that bishops of different countries oversee how the arts are utilized in worship (n. 127) and adapt to what the Constitution calls "the needs and customs of their different regions" (n. 128).

What has therefore occurred in the United States (and in other countries) has been the publication of documents to specify the way the general teachings of the church regarding music can and should be implemented in America. Two documents about music are of particular import: *Music in Catholic Worship* (1972), which is principally about the

Mass, and *Liturgical Music Today* (1982), which is principally about the other sacraments and the Liturgy of the Hours. In these implementation documents we find great respect paid to variety of expression within the cultural diversity of the United States (e.g., African American, Latino and other ethnic groups) at the very same time upholding three standards regarding the suitability of music at liturgy: musical (Is it of good musical quality?), liturgical (Does it serve the needs of the reformed liturgy?) and pastoral (Does it serve the assembly that gathers for worship?).

The "liturgical judgment" just mentioned leads me to the issue of principles about what is suitable for liturgical music today. It is clear from the Liturgy Constitution through the documents governing the reform of the liturgy from Rome plus the specifications of the individual rites themselves that, above all, the key to appropriate music at liturgy is that it be *music that serves the liturgy*. A basic premise throughout all the reform documents is that the texts of the liturgy to be sung should be set to music that is able to be sung by all those who participate. By no means does this mean that the music should be pedestrian or of low quality (In fact, just the opposite is asked for in the musical "judgment" cited above!). But what is at stake is that congregations not be passive or silent at Mass; they should participate through music as much as possible.

Sometimes the question of style interfaces with the question of what is appropriate for liturgy, and then sides can be drawn with people coming down on either side. The optimum situation would be a music style (or styles) that reflects and respects the variety of persons and cultures who gather for Mass, as well as music written to suit the needs of the reformed Mass itself. My own suspicion is that precisely because this is such a tall order, we may well find ourselves disappointed when the music we use at Mass leaves us wanting. That we have a way to go in composing more adequate music for liturgical participation indicates that this remains an agenda for us. But not forgetting how far we have come should be a cause of optimism and hope.

84. What parts of the Mass should be sung?

Your question is very well phrased because it asks what parts *of the Mass* should be sung, indicating precisely the chief aim in the present reform of liturgical music—that the important texts *of the Mass* be sung before any other music is added to the liturgy. Now, taking my lead from what I have already indicated about the relative importance of different parts of the Mass (specifically how important the proclamation of the eucharistic prayer is for the Mass) and in light of the revised Order of Mass as well as the American document *Music in Catholic Worship* I will indicate the relative weight to be given to various parts of the Mass. The order that follows is from *Music in Catholic Worship*, which begins with the most important category and ends with the least important.

Acclamations. These are the alleluia before the gospel and those in the eucharistic prayer ("holy, holy, holy," memorial acclamation, great amen and the doxology to the Lord's Prayer). The rationale here is that these sung acclamations are intrinsic to the Mass and that music underlines their importance. This is especially true of the acclamations that are intrinsic to the eucharistic prayer (see my response to question 58).

Processionals. The entrance (formerly called the introit) and the communion songs are important to accompany the ritual actions of movement during the Mass itself.

Responsorial Psalm. This is the sung response (almost always from the psalms) to the first reading. Singing helps to draw out the meaning of the psalm as it relates to this particular reading. As a kind of musical echo this psalm balances the act of proclamation with prayerful personal appropriation of the text through the psalm.

Ordinary Chants. In the former missal we used the terms "ordinary" and "proper" of the Mass. The ordinary were the fixed texts; the proper chants were those that changed because of the feast or season. In the present terminology, "ordinary chants" refer to the Lord have mercy, Glory to God, Lord's Prayer, Lamb of God and profession of faith. Even here, there is a kind of hierarchy, since the Lamb of God (which accompanies the action of breaking the bread and pouring the consecrated wine) receives greater emphasis than the profession of faith (the recitation of which stands on its own as a liturgical "action"). You will notice a lot of variety here since not every Mass includes a sung Lord have mercy (since other forms of the penitential rite may be used) and the Glory to God is not part of the daily Mass structure (except for special feasts).

Supplementary Songs. These are regarded as less important, one reason for which is that there are no fixed texts for these parts of the Mass. These are the offertory song, the psalm after communion and the recessional.

85. What is the proper role of liturgical music in the Mass?

Succinctly put, the role of music is to enhance the liturgy as a sung and enacted ritual and the more the music supports the act of worship in the Mass the better.

I can remember some of the early debates about the reform of music in the liturgy. The earliest descriptions called for music that was *liturgical*, meaning that it served the rites and the texts, rather than what had commonly been in vogue, namely *music at liturgy*, meaning hymns or other music added on to the Mass. More recently, I think that a better phrase is *musical liturgy*. I say this because this phrase immediately connotes that music is intrinsic to liturgy and that by its nature a generous amount of the liturgy's texts should be sung. The more the nature of the Mass as *musical liturgy* can be appreciated through the wise choice of types of music that can be sung, the better off we are in sustaining the kind of integral vision of music and liturgy, as the documents about the revised liturgy presume.

In addition, I would also say that a judicious use of music can enhance the liturgical experience of festivity and celebration and that this is always an ongoing task because of the nature of the reformed Mass. The principle enunciated in the General Instruction on the Liturgy of the Hours regarding "progressive solemnity" is operative here. This term suggests that given the number of legitimate options for singing in the Mass (and among the various roles of who does the singing: congregation, cantor, choir, schola and so forth) a careful selection from these options can enhance the solemnity of certain celebrations at the same time that it characterizes other occasions as less festive. For example, one might want to enhance the liturgies of the Sundays of the Easter season by emphasizing the singing of the eucharistic acclamations and the Glory to God with particularly robust and festive music, but during the Lenten Sundays an atmosphere of simplicity and directness could be achieved by minimizing the complexity of the music chosen and sung. In fact, some parishes that wish to move away from emphasizing the recessional song (because it is not an intrinsic part *of the Mass*) have chosen Lent as a season when they have no music after the deacon's (or priest's) dismissal. What progressive solemnity offers is a way to choose from a number of options in the Mass and to invite creativity and artistry of musicians who can continue to enhance the kind of participation that the reformed liturgy presumes.

86. Is any religious song okay to sing at a Mass? If not, where do the songs come from? Who picks them?

No, not every religious song is all right for the Mass. Part of the reason is that the emphasis is now placed on singing the texts *of the Mass* itself, not additional music. But this does not mean that there is no room for variety and creativity. For example, even where the missal gives us texts to be sung at the entrance and communion, the Appendix to the General Instruction of the Roman Missal for dioceses of the United States indicates that substitutes are possible. These substitutions include a "song from other collections of psalms and antiphons" or another "sacred song" chosen in light of the function of that particular part of the Mass. This means, for example, that the entrance song should foster a sense of communal participation in the Mass, especially as we come to hear the Word of God. The communion song should foster the sense of community that the pilgrim church expresses as it approaches the reception of the Eucharist in joy and thanksgiving.

Now you may have noticed that I have thus far avoided using the term "hymn" and have preferred the term "song." This is deliberate in order to underscore the freedom for forms of musical expression that is allowable in the present Mass. Sometimes hymns are in fact commonly used at the processions in the Mass. However, the fact that these processions were traditionally accompanied by the singing of psalms reminds us that the Book of Psalms itself is the church's prayer book in the liturgy and that the more we can use these texts in the Mass the more able we are to help people rediscover the depth, complexity and richness of these prayers. In addition, if psalms are chosen as processional chants, this opens up the possibility of having the congregation join in the antiphon while the cantor, schola or choir sings the requisite number of verses of the psalm to accompany the procession. This option might better facilitate the people's participation in singing at communion, because if they sing only the antiphons, they will not need to carry worship aids or worship books in procession, which makes the act of receiving the Eucharist in the hand and from the chalice at least somewhat cumbersome.

Now as to who chooses the music, that's a good but complex question! A lot depends on the structure your parish has for *planning* the whole Mass. Unlike the Tridentine Mass (the structure of which I discussed briefly in question 21), the present missal offers a number of options. These need to be chosen carefully in order that the Mass be conducted in a reverent manner that invites familiarity with its parts for the sake of popular participation. Some of these include choosing the penitential rite, preface, eucharistic prayer, blessing and dismissal, or composing the general intercessions or the announcements at the end of Mass. When these choices have been made, then there is the question of what parts of these are to be sung, as well as the larger issue of appropriate musical settings for the acclamations and other sung texts. Finally, there is the question of what texts and music will be sung to supplement or take the place of what is in the missal (e.g., processional songs). Ideally, there should be some group process at work to choose the various parts of the Mass. Among these there should be significant musical input from those charged with the parish's music ministry. So to the precise question of who decides, I'd have to say that it depends, but that it should not be arbitrary or left only to those who are trained musicians. The issue is no longer to pick the hymns but rather to choose options wisely, both textual and musical, thus enhancing what we celebrate at Mass.

87. What about Latin and Gregorian chant? Can/should we still sing them?

Thank you for a question that serves as a way of describing some features of the present reform of the Mass that derive from earlier church legislation and instruction. You see, the issue of the value and use of Gregorian chant goes back to the document from Pope Pius X in 1903, *Tra le sollecutidini*, in which he took bold leadership in the direction that ultimately led to the kind of liturgy reform that stresses popular participation. In fact, Pope Pius X called for the restoration of the "patrimony of Gregorian chant" for use in the Mass precisely so that the people could take part in the Mass through singing the chant melodies that were simpler than much of the polyphony sung by choirs at the time. To make my point a bit clearer, let's return to the answer to question 83, where I distinguished the issue of appropriate *musical style* from the *ritual requirements of the Mass*. I would also like to reiterate what I suggested there, namely, that the church has never adopted any one style of art (architecture, music and so forth) as its own, but has encouraged many and different kinds of musical styles to be used in the liturgy. Now, given the present emphasis on popular participation in the liturgy itself, what Pius X had to say about chant is quite applicable, both in terms of how it meets the liturgical need of fostering participation and the issue of a desirable style of music. One of the great features of the simple chant style is that it fosters participation even by those untrained in music. Its simplicity made it a desirable way to participate musically in the Latin Mass. Now that the Mass is in the vernacular, the same kind of simple and direct *style* of music would be highly desirable. Whether this means that we sing Gregorian chant as a regular part of the liturgy in our parishes is another matter.

Clearly, one of the advantages of singing Gregorian chant is its universality—these same melodies can be sung throughout the world. Therefore, given the amount of travel that people do today, there is clearly something to be said in favor of retaining some chant pieces in the liturgy. Thus, when traveling and participating in liturgy not in our native language, then at least these parts can serve as familiar vehicles for participation. In addition, recent instructions from Rome regarding music support the preservation of this body of music as an important cultural and liturgical contribution of the Catholic Church. Therefore, one pastoral application of what I have been saying might be to sing the chant as one or another of the ordinary chants of the Mass on a somewhat regular basis. This would afford the kind of sense of universality along with the value of participation through what is simple and direct, both textually and musically.

But I would also like to use this argument about style and the demands of the present liturgy to offer a challenge to contemporary composers of liturgical music. It seems that we have established some sense of familiarity in liturgical participation through music with the rather common use of some settings to the acclamations for the eucharistic prayer, the alleluia, and other prayers. What I think remains an important unfinished agenda item is the composition of a similar kind of familiar (American idiom?) music for the processional chants at the entrance and communion, ideally, based on the psalms. While we have, I think, made significant progress in deepening our participation in and appreciation of the responsorial psalm, I also think that a good bit of work remains to be done on these processional chants. I am not saying that we should do this in order to make this music standard or required (as parts of the chant were in the Tridentine Mass). I am arguing for another vehicle whereby congregations can participate in the Mass by singing psalms set to music that reflects the simplicity, directness and depth of the Gregorian chant.

A last thought. Sometimes the corpus of Gregorian chant is exalted as the "be all and end all" of quality church music. I'd like to offer the thought that a lot of chant texts found their way to the scriptorium floors of many monasteries before the "final" chant book was produced! Trial and error marked the development of that style of sung prayer. Perhaps with a little patience and effort devoted to the principles of the revised Mass, we will someday have a better and more complete repertoire of appropriate music for the vernacular liturgy.

IX.

EUCHARISTIC DOCTRINE AND DISCIPLINE

88. I was taught that the "real presence" was the Eucharist, but today I keep hearing about Christ being present in other things like the scriptures, the assembly and the priest. Can you clarify this for me?

You are quite right about what you were taught: that the Eucharist contains the "real presence" of Christ. But what you are hearing today about Christ being present in many ways is also true. Let's take a theoretical and historical step backward to explain. It may sound a little harsh at first, but when it comes to the church's defined teaching about sacraments throughout its history, it is clear that this body of teaching is relatively small and has been largely reactive. This is to say, when the church faced controversies about the understanding of what the Eucharist was, it then tried to clear up errors and misunderstandings by asserting truths that were clear and precise answers to the errors of the time. Specifically, this means that as the church evolved through the Middle Ages, the term "real presence" came about as a helpful way to assert that Christ was present in the consecrated bread and wine. The controversy that required this definition centered around one Berangarius of Tours (France) in the eleventh century. Later on, when debates about Christ's presence in the Eucharist were renewed in the controversies with the Reformers in the sixteenth century (Luther, Calvin, Zwingli and so forth), the issues were slightly different and the church found itself required to defend the real presence by using the term "transubstantiation." (This means that the *substance* of the bread and wine is changed into the *substance* of Christ's body and blood while the *accidents*, what it looks and tastes like, remain.)

The *Decree on the Holy Eucharist* from the Council of Trent, which responded to the reformers' teachings, contains eight chapters, the first of which is entitled "The Real Presence of Our Lord Jesus Christ in the Most Holy Sacrament of the Eucharist." It is here that we find the phrase that Christ is present "truly, really and substantially." Later on, Trent will also assert that transubstantiation is "a most fitting way" (the Latin word is *aptissime*) to describe the change of bread and wine into the body and blood of Christ. The church relied on these terms for centuries in order to ensure orthodox belief.

However, at Vatican II, because the polemics of the Reformation were no longer the issue at hand, it was judged best to reemphasize other ways that Christ is present in the Eucharist. These issues were never denied by the church, but they had suffered neglect because of the legitimate emphasis on Christ's presence in the bread and wine. In other words, the church once more had the opportunity to reinvent its teaching in light of present theological and pastoral need. So, in the Liturgy Constitution of Vatican II it states that "in the sacrifice of the Mass" that Christ is present "not only in the person of his minister, but especially in the eucharistic elements...[and that] he is present in his word [and] lastly when the Church prays and sings" (n. 7). This is a significant statement, for it refocuses our attention on these other, very traditional ways in which Christ is present to us in the Eucharist. Pope Paul VI reiterated this teaching in his encyclical *Mysterium Fidei* (1965) when he states that "*the real presence* [should] not exclude the other kinds as though they were not real, but because it is real par excellence, since it is substantial, in the sense that Christ whole and entire, God and man, becomes present." These statements are summarized in the document from the Vatican's Congregation of Rites in 1965 *(Eucharisticum Mysterium)* when it speaks about the *modes* of Christ's presence: in the assembly of the faithful, in his word, in the person of the minister and "above all in the eucharistic elements" (n. 9). Now you may ask, why does the mode of Christ in the elements still seem to receive greater emphasis? Well, the fact remains that Catholic doctrine, precisely defined at Trent, did place great emphasis on Christ's presence in the eucharistic elements of bread and wine, and this should not be lost in contemporary descriptions. The church's liturgical texts describe Christ's presence in the General Instruction of the Roman Missal by stating that "Christ is really present to the assembly gathered in his name; he is present in the person of the minister, in his own word and indeed substantially and permanently under the eucharistic elements."

If I were to try to summarize the church's teaching, I'd say that Christ is present in the Eucharist and that in trying to explain the *ways* he is present to the church, I'd emphasize four: assembly, word, species and minister. I find the word "modes" very useful when discussing Christ's presence because it emphasizes *that Christ himself is present in various ways*. A good human analogy may be how we humans are "present" to each other—through words, gestures and signs of relationship or affection. Just as we use words and gestures to express our relationship to each other, so it is through the Liturgy of the Eucharist that the church uses words, gestures and signs to communicate the one presence of Christ with us in varied ways. Christ is present where "two or three are gathered in [his] name" (Mt 18:20), through the spoken speech of the proclaimed scriptures, through the action of the transformation and communion in the bread and wine become the body and blood of Christ, and through the ordained minister acting in the very person of Christ. Through all of this discussion we realize that Christ's intimate and personal commitment to the church is realized and expressed through the whole Liturgy of the Eucharist.

89. Is it true that in a recent survey of American Catholics, most said that they did not believe that at Mass the bread and wine are changed into the body and blood of Christ?

As I thought about framing an answer to your question I realized that I was thinking like a theologian but that I would probably sound like a lawyer when I answered it! I say this because I think lawyers are noted for care with words and language, and your question requires that I exercise great care in discussing the language used in the survey and the summary results that have been popularized.

First, to the survey itself. In late May and early June 1994, Peter Steinfels edited a four-part series of articles in the *New York Times* about the Catholic Church in America. In the last of the articles (June 1, 1994), he summarized the results of a *New York Times/CBS News* poll subtitled "American Catholics: A Church Divided." It is important to examine the exact wording of the question used in the poll and the proposed answers you ask about. The text of the survey asks: "At the Mass, are the bread and wine changed into the body and blood of Christ" or are they "symbolic reminders of Christ?" What concerns me (and others such as Father Avery Dulles in his letter to the *Times*) is the way this issue is framed. When you put the word "change" and "symbolic reminders ' in opposition, I think you are separating what in our theological tradition is really inseparable. For example, throughout this book I have been careful to use the word "memorial" and the command "do this in memory of me" in a positive way. I have also indicated that for a good part of our tradition on eucharistic teaching the terms "symbol" and "sign" have been very important. The church uses them to make sure that the presence of Christ in the Eucharist is understood to be qualitatively different from the normal, physical notion of presence that we use. In effect, the church's teaching about the Eucharist was and is always couched in sacramental and "sign" language. Therefore, when I read that in this poll one had to choose between "change" and the very useful terms "symbolic" and "reminders," then I question the usefulness of the poll itself. As it stands, I would choose the first answer: "changed into the body and blood," but I really would have preferred a different set of choices. (If I sound like a lawyer parsing words, remember that I warned you!)

The second part of your question concerns which percentage said what, and refers to the opinion of the majority. The poll was broken down into age categories: 18–29, 30–44, 45–64 and 65 and older. For those in the first two categories (18–44) roughly 30 percent chose "changed into the body and blood," whereas 70 percent chose "symbolic reminders." For those 45–64, the percentages shifted so that 37 percent chose "changed into the body and blood" and 58 percent chose "symbolic reminders." It was only a majority of those 65 or older who chose "changed into the body and blood" (51 percent) over "symbolic reminders" (45 percent). Obviously, on the face of these numbers we have something to be very concerned about! But at the same time, given the difficulty that I see in the wording of the question, I am not really surprised that only those 65 and older find the second choice about "symbolic reminders" deficient. After all, they were raised in the pre–Vatican II years, when Catholic theological principles were most often phrased as antidotes to Protestant errors. Their emphasis on "symbol" was seen to be wrong and Catholics felt the need to assert what was *really real* about the Eucharist. My only thought is that perhaps those who chose "symbolic reminders" were responding in a way that validated what we have emphasized since Vatican II in theology and the liturgy of the Mass, namely, that the Eucharist is an act of memory and that we engage in symbolic (and yes, also very real) actions that draw us into the mystery of Christ's saving death and resurrection.

I'd say we should do two things. First, we should take this poll at face value and realize its flaws in language. It separated "change" from "symbol/memorial," which to my mind cannot be separated. Second, we should make sure that, when appropriate through the range of education programs and opportunities, we emphasize the active and real modes of the presences of Christ (as described in the previous answer) so that we can firmly reiterate the fullness of Catholic teaching about the presence of Christ at Mass.

90. What makes our teaching on the Eucharist different from that of other churches?

I suspect that I might have had an easier job answering your prob-ing question before Vatican II rather than now! I say this because much of our Catholic doctrine on the Eucharist was determined at the Council of Trent because of the controversies at the time of the Reformation. The lan-guage of that council was definitive and often described Catholic teaching over against what others taught. In fact, much of the language of the decrees of Trent stated "…if anyone teaches [a named error] let him/her be condemned." In their legitimate concern to support traditional Catholic teaching, the bishops at Trent took positions that were often diametrically opposed to those of the reformers about the Eucharist as sacrifice, com-munion under two species and other such issues. Where Martin Luther firmly taught that the Eucharist was a gift from God (a *beneficium*), it could not be a sacrifice *(sacrificium)*. This led the council fathers to state explicitly and fully that the Eucharist was indeed a sacrifice (session 22, September 1562, canons 1738–60). Similarly, when the bishops at Trent faced the reformers' insistence that one had to receive both the eucharistic bread and cup at Mass, they turned to the commonly held doctrine of *con-comitance*. This doctrine, which teaches that one could receive Christ by partaking of the eucharistic bread only, was thus asserted at Trent (session 21, July 1562, canons 1725–34).

After the Council of Trent, the church issued a *Catechism*, summa-rizing the chief teachings of the council in a useful question-and-answer format. This led to the eventual publication of American versions of the cat-echism for use in educational programs in America (called *The Baltimore Catechism*). Therefore, what American Catholics were commonly taught before Vatican II was a set of teachings asserting our beliefs over against those of the reformers (most often grouped together as "Protestants"). So it is not surprising that Catholics asserted their belief in Christ's real pres-ence in the Mass, that they called the change in bread and wine "transub-stantiation," that the Eucharist was indeed a sacrifice, and that one need receive only the species of the eucharistic bread, not both bread and cup, to receive Christ.

At Vatican II the church sought to reemphasize its core teachings in a more pastoral, invitational way and strove to distinguish what we held to as Catholic beliefs from what *seemed* to be a part of that core set of beliefs: to separate *what* we believed from *the way it was expressed*.

Since Vatican II there has been a reemphasis on the four presences of Christ at Mass—not just language about the real presence in the eucharistic species of consecrated bread and wine. Also, Vatican II marked the beginning of a reemphasis on the power and efficaciousness of Christ's presence through the proclaimed word, which was certainly something we Catholics shied away from after Trent. Also, given the increased opportunities that we Catholics have today to receive both species, our traditional doctrine of concomitance, while not changed or revised, remains in place but is certainly not emphasized as it was after Trent.

In addition, given the ecumenical climate ushered in at Vatican II, there is a whole new way of looking at issues about the Mass, not just in terms of what "we" and "they" teach, but what we can affirm together and what we still need to dialogue about more fully. This leads me to think not only in terms of what makes our teaching about the Eucharist "different" from other churches, but also to realize that sometimes today what we are dealing with are *degrees of difference*. Hence, for example, as Catholics we assert that the Eucharist is a sacrifice, the same sacrifice of Jesus at Calvary. Today most churches dating from the Reformation teach that to some degree at least, the Eucharist is the sacrifice of Jesus. What makes our teachings different today on this issue is a matter of degree. Similarly, when it comes to asserting our belief in the real presence of Christ in the Eucharist, we Catholics have traditionally used transubstantiation, but we are able to use other terms. (Recall what I said regarding Pope Paul VI's assertion in *Eucharisticum Mysterium* that, provided we sustain the meaning of the term "transubstantiation" we can develop new terminology to describe the Eucharist that contemporary Catholics may find easier to comprehend.) Many Protestants never liked this term because it was unbiblical and yet some eventually used "consubstantiation" (meaning that Christ was present *with* the bread and wine) to distinguish their teaching from ours. Today I'd say that the vast majority of the Christian churches prefer the biblical language, "This is my body...blood," and much Catholic teaching today uses the same phrasing.

Does this mean that we all now believe the same things about the Eucharist? No. But it does mean that we need to be very careful and exacting when we describe what we believe and the way these points are phrased. It also means that we Catholics have some practices that are not shared by other churches, such as acts of reverence to the Eucharist during the liturgy or when the eucharistic bread is reserved after

Mass. The current ecumenical climate has also helped us to restore practices that were never condemned but that seemed to be "non-Catholic,"
such as Mass in the vernacular, people participating in the whole Mass
and the Eucharist given under two species. We Catholics have regained
this territory, which Protestants never surrendered at the Reformation.

Allow me to say at least a word about how we Catholics have
gained insight into eucharistic teaching from the Eastern churches. Their
emphasis on the role of the Holy Spirit in all liturgy and their emphasis on
the invocation of the Holy Spirit through the prayer called the epiclesis have
helped us Catholics reemphasize the way the Spirit acts in our liturgy.
From Trent on, this was a silent part of our traditional teaching. The
revived epicletic prayers in much of the revised liturgy have helped us to
readdress this neglected but nonetheless very traditional and important
part of our liturgy and theology.

91. How can the real presence of our Lord continue in the bread and wine after the eucharistic celebration has ended?

I suspect that there are a number of ways of answering your intrigu-
ing question. But allow me to offer two approaches, one philosophical
and the other in light of the church's practice. I call the first part of this
answer philosophical because it has to do with what is real as a result of
human actions and speech. When the priest prays the eucharistic prayer,
especially when he invokes the Holy Spirit in the epiclesis and uses the
words of Jesus from the scriptures, "This is my body…blood," what he is
doing is declaring the bread and wine to be the body and blood of Christ.
He does this not on his own initiative or because of his personal power. He
performs this action at God's gracious invitation and acts "in the person of
Christ" at Mass, not in his own person alone. But what is at stake here is
a prayer that invokes God's almighty power. When we speak in the Mass,
something happens, and that "something" is an act of God, transforming
gifts into Christ's body and blood and changing us who share in the
Eucharist into more complete reflections of Christ in the world. When we
use the words of Christ, bread and wine change, become something they
were not before; they are now our nourishment for the journey to eternal
life. When this transformed bread and wine are eaten and drunk, they are
truly our act of communion—with God in Christ and with each other. But
even if they are not consumed then and there, they remain what they have

become through God's power and will. They don't revert to their former nature. They are what they have become and remain the body and blood of Christ. What the spoken words effected in the eucharistic change continues even after the Mass has ended. Or, in the words of the philosopher, "What is, is."

Now to the practice of the church. From the earliest records we have of the primitive eucharistic celebrations (second and third century), it is clear that the whole assembly shared in both the consecrated bread and wine. It is also equally clear that when the Mass ended, deacons were sent forth to distribute the eucharistic elements to those who were absent because of ill health, age or other reasons. This means that the church's practice presumed that the eucharistic elements of Christ's body and blood remained precisely that after the Mass ended. The eucharistic action led to eucharistic distribution after Mass. This also led to the church reserving the eucharistic species in a safe place so that it could be taken to those near death (as *viaticum*). Logically, this led to the practice that because the Eucharist was reserved for the communion of the sick, it was adored through acts of devotion. But again, all this developed because of the belief that what happened at Mass truly transformed bread and wine into Christ's body and blood. What was effected through God's power could not be undone.

92. Who may receive communion? Specifically, what should happen at weddings and funerals when non-Catholics and nonpracticing Catholics are present and it's time for communion?

Your question is one of the most sensitive that regularly surface in pastoral practice. In fact, a friend of mine who conducts a weekly session for inquirers about the Catholic faith (which leads to some participants becoming catechumens and eventually baptized Catholics) repeatedly tells me that this is the most frequently asked question at those meetings, and the one that causes the greatest controversy. As she says, on the one hand, the church wants to be invitational about sharing the Eucharist by encouraging regular reception of communion; but on the other hand, it limits who can come to the eucharistic table.

What is going on here has a number of levels of meaning, and they need careful explanation. The issue about who may receive has deep roots, is complex and has much more to do with what we believe in general and the meaning of church belonging than the particular act of taking communion at Mass. Let me start by noting that the Eucharist is a sacrament of initiation and, in fact, is the sacrament that ends the act of sacramental initiation for adults at Easter (water baptism, confirmation and Eucharist). The theological principle here is that one must first be baptized (and adults must also be confirmed) before they can receive the Eucharist. The reason is that one needs to make an act of faith in the triune God, Father, Son and Spirit; be immersed in the living waters of the baptismal font (or have water poured on them); and be anointed with the chrism of salvation with the seal of the Holy Spirit. All of this is the church's liturgical way of celebrating our new life in Christ, which is then ratified and renewed every time we celebrate the Eucharist. This means that while the church is invitational and wants all to receive new life in Christ, it also insists that we be members of Christ's body through baptism and confirmation before we share in the sacred meal of the Eucharist. As early as the thanksgiving prayer from the *Didache*, the church verbalizes its position: "Let no one eat or drink of your eucharist except those baptized in the name of the Lord. 'Do not give what is holy to dogs'" (Mt 7:6).

Now the question arises, who is baptized and what does it mean to belong to the church? Contemporary church teaching recognizes that baptisms in non–Roman Catholic Christian churches that are performed with water (immersing or pouring) and with the invocation of the Trinity (Father, Son and Holy Spirit) are true baptisms and make one a member of the household of Christ. But does this automatically mean that the recipients of such baptisms can share in the Eucharist? No. And it is here that the plot thickens.

The principal reason why not everyone whose baptism is recognized as valid can share in our Eucharist has to do with the church's teachings about the Eucharist itself and about who presides at the Mass. For non-Catholics to think about coming to share in our Eucharist, they first must believe what the church teaches about the real presence of Christ in the sacrament. In addition, the priest who presides at Mass must be validly ordained in a church with apostolic succession; that is, his ordination line can be traced back to the first apostles. This is often where the problem arises. Not every church from the time of the Reformation espoused the value of the hierarchy (bishops, priests, deacons). Rather, some insisted on a comparatively egalitarian idea of liturgical leadership and church government. We Catholics are accustomed to the hierarchy and know that the body of bishops in the church are our doctrinal and spiritual leaders. Their authority in these matters comes from the first apostles, and the tradition that they received from Christ is handed on to succeeding generations in the church. This way of understanding the authority of bishops and the value of ordination by bishops in apostolic succession is not universally held in non–Roman Catholic Christian churches. It is essentially for this reason that Catholics cannot say that the Eucharist of other churches is the same as ours. For example, this would mean that we would recognize the validity of the ordination of priests in the Eastern churches, but not in all Protestant churches because of what they believe or don't believe about ordination.

This brings me to another distinction having to do with unity in belief systems. From the time of the Crusades on (the eleventh century), preexisting tensions between Eastern and Western Christians progressed to a breaking point. Today, while there is a substantial ground of common teaching and belief, there is a clear separation between us. The causes of this separation stem from both sides. Some of the issues concern the way we describe who Christ is and the authority of the pope and Rome in relation to other church leaders (patriarchs). Certainly, the contemporary East-West dialogues regarding theology and sacraments have helped move us toward more complete unity, but we are not there yet. This fosters a situation in which all the baptized do not share in the same set of beliefs, causing us to not invite members of other Christian churches to the Eucharist, under normal conditions. This set of practices is summarized for us in the present Code of Canon Law (especially n. 844).

There are exceptions to this position in cases of necessity, and this is where the issues become more complex. The Canon Law states that in cases of true necessity (e.g., danger of death, no ordained priest available and so forth) that a Catholic may request Eucharist, penance and anointing of the sick "from non-Catholic ministers in whose churches these sacraments are valid." Similarly, a member of an oriental (Eastern) church in these same circumstances may request these sacraments from a Catholic priest. Catholic priests may also administer the Eucharist, penance and anointing to members of another Christian church "provided they manifest Catholic faith in these sacraments and be properly disposed." In general, we may say that sharing in the Eucharist means much more than that. It includes sharing in "faith, worship and ecclesial life" (from the 1993 *Directory for Ecumenism*, Pontifical Council for Promoting Christian Unity, Rome).

Our American bishops are aware of the complexity and real pastoral importance of this issue. Therefore, in November 1996 they approved the following set of guidelines for the reception of communion (which replaced the guidelines they had approved in 1986 to reflect the 1993 *Directory for Ecumenism* from Rome). It's very likely that you are aware of these guidelines as they appear in most worship aids. They state:

For Catholics:

As Catholics, we fully participate in the celebration of the Eucharist when we receive Holy Communion. We are encouraged to receive Communion devoutly and frequently. In order to be properly disposed to receive Communion, participants should not be conscious of grave sin and normally should have fasted for one hour. A person who is conscious of grave sin is not to receive the Body and Blood of the Lord without prior sacramental confession except for a grave reason where there is no opportunity for confession. In this case, the person is to be mindful of the obligation to make an act of perfect contrition, including the intention of confessing as soon as possible (Canon 916). A frequent reception of the Sacrament of Penance is encouraged for all.

For our fellow Christians:

We welcome our fellow Christians to this celebration of the Eucharist as our brothers and sisters. We pray that our common baptism and the action of the Holy Spirit in this Eucharist will draw us closer to one another and begin to dispel the sad divisions which separate us. We pray that these will lessen and finally disappear, in keeping with Christ's prayer for us "that they may be one" (Jn 17:21).

Because Catholics believe that the celebration of the Eucharist is a sign of the reality of the oneness of faith, life and worship, members of those churches with whom we are not yet fully united are ordinarily not admitted to Holy Communion. Eucharistic sharing in exceptional circumstances by other Christians requires permission according to the directives of the diocesan bishop and the provisions of canon law (Canon 844.4). Members of the Orthodox Churches, the Assyrian Church of the East and the Polish National Catholic

Church are urged to respect the discipline of their own Churches. According to Roman Catholic discipline, the Code of Canon Law does not object to the reception of communion by Christians of these Churches (Canon 844.3).

For those not receiving Holy Communion:
All who are not receiving Holy Communion are encouraged to express in their hearts a prayerful desire for unity with the Lord Jesus and with one another.

For non-Christians:
We also welcome to this celebration those who do not share our faith in Jesus Christ. While we cannot admit them to Holy Communion, we ask them to offer their prayers for the peace and unity of the human family.

Normally, we share communion with others in the same church who profess the same beliefs (particularly regarding the Eucharist and ordination). In cases of true necessity certain conditions must be met, including at least substantial unity in belief. We should never seek to proselytize or change another's belief; we may, however, invite them to understand Roman Catholic beliefs and practices. What I see as the real difficulty here is that we don't always appreciate that sharing eucharistic communion, sharing beliefs and belonging to the church are all interrelated. These are of a piece, and we should strive to deepen that awareness that you can't have one without the others.

93. Can someone receive communion more than once in a day? Under what conditions?

The traditional discipline of the church has been that one can receive the Eucharist only once per day. This teaching was reiterated in 1973 in a Vatican document "on facilitating reception of communion in certain circumstances" (the Latin title is *Immensae Caritatis*). However, in addition to reiterating the once-per-day norm, the document goes on to state certain circumstances when a person may receive communion more than once a day. In general, the instruction is that one may receive more than once at a Mass for special circumstances, and that one may not receive more than once simply for devotional reasons. One may receive more than once a day on the following occasions: at ritual Masses, that is, when a sacrament is celebrated (baptism, confirmation, ordination and so forth); at a Mass for the consecration of a church or altar; at a Mass for the dead (funeral, anniversary and so forth); on the occasion of a bishop's or a major superior's visitation; at a Mass marking a special spiritual congress, meeting, or pilgrimage; and, finally, family members and friends at a Mass when viaticum is administered to a dying person.

94. If I choose not to receive communion during Mass, do I still fulfill my Sunday obligation?

The direct answer is yes. Sunday obligation requires that we participate in the Mass, but it does not specify that one must receive communion. However, the value of receiving communion on a regular basis was first recalled in the modern era by Pope Pius X, who urged frequent reception (and lowered the age for first communion to that "of reason"). In addition, the church has traditionally underscored the value of receiving communion during the Easter season. This is called Easter duty (or the eucharistic precept). Because of the importance of celebrating the sacraments of initiation at the Easter vigil, it is not surprising that the church paid special attention to celebrating the Eucharist during the whole fifty days of the Easter season. In 1215, at the Fourth Lateran Council, it was decreed that Catholics had to receive communion at least once during this season. The contemporary application of this is in the present (1983) Code of Canon Law, which specifies this obligation during the time from Passion (Palm) Sunday through Pentecost. In the United States, this period has been extended from the first Sunday of Lent to Trinity Sunday (the Sunday after Pentecost). One ecumenical note is worth mentioning. It was not uncommon for many Christian churches not to celebrate the Eucharist every Sunday, but instead to celebrate a Liturgy of the Word, with the sermon as a central element of the rite. What has happened in the past thirty or so years is that the Catholic insistence on the Eucharist being celebrated every Sunday has been adopted by Protestant churches, which now see great value in this traditional practice.

95. Why has the time of fast before receiving communion changed?

Let me offer an overview of the origins of the fast and what this discipline has meant in our tradition. One of the first indications we have regarding the nature of the earliest celebrations of the Eucharist is from St. Paul in his First Letter to the Corinthians (chapter 11). In it he addresses abuses of the practice of celebrating the Lord's Supper within an actual meal, specifically the worshipers' failure to share food with each other. It is not surprising that the Eucharist and its meal setting eventually became separated, and as early as the third and fourth centuries we have evidence that Christians were to abstain from food and drink (e.g., wine) for some period of time before receiving the Eucharist. The modern legislation on the required eucharistic fast stems from Pius XII. Before his pontificate, people had to fast from all solid food and drink (except water) from midnight until they received the Eucharist. Pius XII changed the time to three hours. Under the pontificate of Paul VI, the length of the fast was decreased to one hour. This norm applies today. Paul VI's decision came as a direct result of the request of many bishops, who noted the difficulty some people had in maintaining the eucharistic fast. Exceptions to this norm extend to the sick, who may take any food and medicine they need up to the time of receiving communion (reiterated in the 1973 document *Immensae Caritatis*). From a pastoral standpoint, these recent papal decisions enable people to participate in the Mass at various times of the day, especially in the evening. In addition, the mitigation of any fast for the sick enables them to receive communion whenever possible. This is especially useful today, given the numbers of eucharistic ministers we have. This ministry of taking the Eucharist to the sick and the homebound reflects the important link that the church has always made between the table of the Lord in church and serving the Lord in each other.

As with any other act of fasting, there are a number of spiritual values associated with this practice. One is that we abstain from food and drink so that our senses are not dulled; this fosters participation with greater attention and alertness. (In the third-century document from Hippolytus, the *Apostolic Tradition*, we read that those being initiated at the Easter vigil had to fast, and that at the time of communion they also received a mixture of milk and honey to break their fast and to help sustain them until they could eat after the ceremony.) Another benefit is that when we fast we deny ourselves nourishment so that others may use what we do not eat for their nourishment. The food we deny ourselves can (should?) become food for the poor and needy.

Now the rationale as to why the eucharistic fast has been so clearly mitigated over the past forty years is simply to allow more people to share in communion more frequently. In our century, there has been unprecedented papal encouragement that we receive the Eucharist as often as possible (beginning with Pius X in the early years of this century); mitigating the fast is another clear example of this encouragement.

96. Is it ever acceptable to receive communion at a service that isn't Roman Catholic? Is it equivalent to Catholic communion?

In replying to question 92, I tried to summarize the cluster of issues that surround sharing communion with people of other Christian faiths. Your specific question is addressed in the present Code of Canon Law (Canon 844. 2). Because of the importance of this tersely worded norm, let me quote it in full:

> Whenever necessity requires, or genuine spiritual advantage suggests, and provided that the danger of error or indifferentism is avoided, it is lawful for the faithful for whom it is physically or morally impossible to approach a Catholic minister, to receive the sacraments of Penance, Eucharist and Anointing of the Sick from non-Catholic ministers in whose churches these sacraments are valid.

First of all, this norm underscores the public action that Eucharist always is by insisting that there be no question of scandalizing anyone by our actions, either because they might misunderstand our belief in what the Eucharist is or fail to realize what church we belong to. Next is the question of the impossibility of approaching a Catholic minister. This means that we would not go to communion at a non-Catholic Christian wedding, funeral or such simply because of courtesy. If there is a Catholic church nearby, we are to attend our own church for distribution of the sacraments. However, if a person is near death or in a location where there is no Catholic church or priest—while on vacation, for example—then we may approach a non-Catholic minister provided that the last stipulation is met, namely, that these sacraments are considered valid by Roman Catholics. This norm is reiterated in the 1993 *Directory for Ecumenism* (from the Pontifical Council for Promoting Christian Unity), which same document underscores our closeness with the Eastern churches and that, given situations of necessity, we may approach them for sacraments. What remains unspecified, however, is precisely what other churches this norm might refer to. The concrete issue for American Catholics is which Protestant churches this might include, now or in the future. I suspect this to be deliberately left open in this text because the Vatican is engaged in high-level discussions with a number of Christian churches (Anglicans, Lutherans, Methodists and so forth) on international and national levels about matters of doctrine and practice. The church's general norms as stated in canon law and this *Directory* leave open the possibility of our drawing together on matters of faith and practice. The United States bishops faced this question in 1986 and again in 1996, when they issued *Guidelines for Communion Reception*, which I've quoted in full in my answer to question 92. It is a succinct pastoral instruction for our country, drafted to meet our particular needs.

Certainly pain and personal suffering surround these issues, especially when we face the lack of unity in faith within our own families. The stance of the Catholic Church since Vatican II has been far more open and invitational than in the years preceding it. However, when the norms underscore the importance of avoiding "indifferentism," it suggests that "free and easy access" to the sacraments of other Christian churches is not envisioned and is not to be fostered. Hence, when attending weddings and funerals under normal circumstances in other churches, we are to refrain from receiving communion because we do not share the fullness of faith with them. When I was growing up, I often heard the phrase, "The family that prays together, stays together." At least partially, what the church's present legislation on communion underscores is the concept that "The family that believes together shares communion together." Note that I used the terms "family" and "together." Because we share common beliefs, we share a common eucharistic table.

Now our sharing in communion is not meant to signify that we are perfect, totally united or sinless—far from it! After all, if we were, we wouldn't need sacraments in the first place. The issue here is whether we have a sufficient degree of belonging to one another within the church so as to share in communion, thus making our belief less imperfect and our common life less disunited. One of the purposes of the Mass is to help us become less and less imperfect as God's pilgrim church on earth. But it is because we go to God together in the meantime, in the church, that we share faith and sacraments with one another—a communion of people who share the same faith. The scandal of a disunited Christianity hits home, especially in the area of this sensitive issue. Our annual week of prayer for Christian unity at the end of January (18–25) and occasional ecumenical services of the word stand as continual reminders that we still need to strive for that perfect unity for which Jesus prayed: "…that all may be one."

97. Today, many priests invite everybody to receive holy communion during funerals and weddings, even if the congregation includes non-Catholics or Catholics that do not receive the sacraments regularly or attend Mass weekly. Can you explain?

I think I have answered at least part of your question (about non-Catholics) in replying to the previous question. In addition, I'd like to point to the *Guidelines for Communion Reception*, drafted by the United States bishops in 1996 (found in my answer to question 92), which takes into consideration Catholics, "fellow Christians" and "non-Christians." When addressing Catholics specifically, these guidelines state that one "should not be conscious of grave sin," that a person who is conscious of grave sin "is not to receive the body and blood of the Lord without prior sacramental confession," but if there is no such opportunity, the individual has "the obligation to make an act of perfect contrition, including the intention of confessing as soon as possible." I think you will agree that these norms are clear and are worded in a pastorally sensitive way.

But the pastoral reality is a bit more complex. The percentage of American Catholics who say they are Catholic and who participate in Sunday Mass is somewhere around one-third of those who should be participating. This means that far more Catholics are choosing *not* to celebrate Mass than who choose to do so. Is their lack of attendance a grave sin? Our tradition says that it is. In practice, I suspect that many no longer think that way. (Whether this *should* be what they think is another matter.) So what happens at the pastorally sensitive situations created at weddings and funerals is that many Catholics who do not regularly participate at Sunday Mass choose to receive communion. Some priests I know try to face into this situation by offering to hear confessions after a Christian wake service or after a wedding rehearsal. On the other hand, given the severe decline of priests, it is often enough the case that wake services and wedding rehearsals are conducted by other persons (deacons or laypersons) so that this pastoral "solution" is not always possible. In addition, this same phenomenon of the lessening of the number of priests has itself contributed to the decline in the frequency of sacramental penance. With fewer priests available, fewer people avail themselves of confession.

What is clearly the intention of the American bishops in issuing these guidelines is that they be printed in worship aids and made available for catechesis, so that people are aware of church teaching and practice, especially on these pastorally sensitive occasions. There is nothing to suggest that priests should announce to the whole assembly that everyone is invited to communion. Such a statement goes against the fundamental norm of personal conscience—one makes judgments about one's soul and life before God. That a priest would make a general announcement takes this choice away from an individual. Hopefully, the published guidelines will help people come to terms with the issue of the frequency of their Mass participation and their use of the sacrament of penance.

X.

THE EUCHARIST AND DAILY LIFE

98. I used to love the Tridentine Mass because it marked a special time between God and me. Now, with all the emphasis on participation, I feel that it is a less sacred and holy time. Can you help me?

In responding to the questions in section III on the reform of the liturgy (as well as in other places), I have tried to explain why the Mass has changed, using church documents and the missal itself. Your question hits at some of these issues, so I'd ask you to refer back to those responses. But what I'd like to do here is to frame an answer that deals with your phrase about the Mass as a "sacred and holy time." Certainly, the prescribed rituals of the Tridentine Mass fostered a sense of otherness, splendor and pageantry. The formality of the Mass, the colors and designs of vestments, regular use of incense at high and solemn Masses and Latin chant music all played a part in fostering our appreciation of the Mass as something out of the ordinary, an otherworldly spectacle that afforded us an opportunity to experience the Eucharist as a miracle that depended on God's overarching and sustaining grace. While we know we are unworthy of this gift, the Tridentine rite certainly underscored the distance and separation between us humans and God's infinite holiness.

None of this was wrong, and much of this helped people experience the Mass as a "sacred and holy time." But there were some elements of the Tridentine Mass that the highest church authority and the best of liturgical scholars argued should be changed. In addressing the primary goal of this present reform, the bishops at Vatican II repeatedly cited "full, conscious and active participation" as a chief goal of the changes in the liturgy ushered in with the council. Now in the implementation of the reformed liturgy, I suspect that a great deal has happened that has upset people and caused a disturbance in their experience of the utter transcendence and otherness of God that they had come to experience in the Tridentine Mass. But to be honest, I have to say that some of this may not be bad. As Christians we believe in many paradoxes, not the least of which is God's total otherness and yet, through Christ especially, God's immediate closeness to us, as one of us in his human nature. Similarly, the Mass is supposed to reflect both the transcendence and immanence of

God. If in fact the Tridentine rite emphasized God's transcendence, one of the legitimate criticisms made against it was that it was so otherworldly that it was not a vehicle for adequate participation, comprehension and appropriation into daily life. So I would argue that the purpose of revising the liturgy is well served if there is an emphasis on God's closeness to us, and especially through the vernacular prayers and readings, that we might comprehend them and seek to fulfill them by what we say and do both during the Mass and in daily life itself. In a sense then, based on the kind of God we believe in and pray to at Mass, it is not really appropriate to look to the Mass as a "sacred and holy time" that is removed from daily life. It is better to see the rites and prayers, sounds and rhythms of the liturgy as a special, unique and powerful experience of God, transcendent and immanent, but an experience that draws us into deeper contact with God in daily life.

For me, a useful example from the scriptures to describe what the Mass is meant to be comes from the event of the transfiguration. The disciples ascend a high mountain, experience the word of revelation and see the transfigured Christ, only to leave the mountain and to descend back to daily life sustained and uplifted by that experience. The disciples did not remain on the mountain forever. Nor should we view the act of liturgy as the only place we discover God's sacredness and holiness. We do indeed experience it at Mass, but we also are then encouraged to discover God in daily life as well—and whenever we discover God, it is a "sacred and holy" thing.

Parts of the Mass foster this sense of interrelationship, for example, the general intercessions and the sign of peace. In fact the intercessions were not a part of the Tridentine Mass, and when the sign of peace was exchanged in the former rite it was among the ministers in the sanctuary only. Now that both of these segments have been restored, they serve as important vehicles for the linking of liturgy with life, connecting our experience of God at Mass with the expression of God's mercy and love toward one another. Although many saw the reintroduction of the sign of peace as a severe interruption in the solemnity of the Mass, its meaning (as described by St. Augustine and countless others) ratifies who we are and what we are about at Mass and in life.

99. How does celebrating Mass on Sunday relate to/connect with daily Christian life during the week?

I hinted at this in replying to the previous question. Your question allows me to deepen what I said there and to add to it. I think it was the composer Jerome Kern who wrote the song "Two Different Worlds We Live In." I don't want to disparage this piece of music or the sentiment of the song, but I do want to take issue with this as a way of looking at the Christian life or as a way of describing how the sacred and the secular are separable and separated parts of the Christian life.

In fact we live in *one* world, a world God loved so much that he sent his Son into it to save us by becoming one of us. Thus, we should not view the Mass as a refuge from life. Rather, we should see it as a matrix, a place where the concerns of daily life intersect with God's transcendence and immanence. The whole dynamic of gathering for Mass is that we come together in order to go our separate ways when it has ended. In preparing for Mass, I'd suggest that we pray over the scriptures that will be proclaimed and reflect on the events of our lives and the lives of those we love before coming together to participate. This kind of reflective prayer is crucial in order that what the liturgy presumes to happen will happen: that what we pray be reflective of what we believe and what we live outside of the liturgy. To amplify on the traditional phrase, "The law of prayer establishes the law of belief," I'd like to say that what we pray and what we celebrate together should have a direct impact on how we evaluate life and conduct our daily lives.

Among the many places where the Mass articulates this belief are the following: in the general intercessions, in the presentation of gifts and when eucharistic ministers (and deacons) take communion from the Mass to those who cannot attend and in the dismissal at the end of Mass. In stating the general intercessions the needs of the community are summarized in prayer. We offer our own needs and we are stretched to include the needs of others. What we bring forward as gifts for the Mass—bread, wine, monetary gifts—should reflect our daily lives and our very selves. We present bread and wine, the products of human manufacture, and these gifts become the means for our sharing in the body and blood of Christ. They also reflect human work—what we do "outside," in human labor, has a deep bearing on what we bring to Mass. (In the words of Cardinal Basil Hume: "No work, no Mass.") When ministers bring the Eucharist to the homebound we send them with our prayers. The prayers that the ministers use on these occasions reflect and recall our prayers at Mass for those who could not be with us. Finally, the dismissal rite itself is designed to make these connections. Any announcements at the end of the Mass serve to make the connection between liturgy and daily parish concerns. And the dismissal itself, "Go in peace," or "Go in peace to love and serve the Lord," capsulizes much of what the Mass is about—living what we have shared through God's grace and love.

Another significant example of this intrinsic link between liturgy and daily life and a reminder that we live in *one* graced world is the restoration of the diaconate as a permanent liturgical ministry. In all of the revised rites since Vatican II, the role of the deacon is presumed as a constitutive part of every liturgical rite. The restoration of this ministry is not just for the sake of the liturgy—it is also for the sake of diaconal service outside of the liturgy. As I have argued before, the deacon served as the central minister who bridged worship and social ministry. It was the deacon who served at the Lord's table because he served the hungry from foodstuffs collected at Mass. It was the deacon who proclaimed the gospel and it was the deacon who preached the gospel by words and more poignantly by the kind of passion he exhibited for the spreading of God's justice in the world. It was the deacon who proclaimed the intercessions because it was he through his ministry in the community who came to know of those who were sick or in special need. The restoration of this ministry in the church is especially significant because it is the deacon who acts as Christ the servant at the table of the Lord at Mass and at the table of those most in need, the poor. Therefore, much is at stake when deacons function liturgically and minister in the life of the church. They personify and exemplify the fact that we live in one graced world…not "two different worlds."

100. I hear the phrase "liturgical spirituality" but don't know what it means. Does it refer to the Mass in any way(s)?

There are several ways to approach your very crucial question— I say crucial because unless we deepen our appreciation of liturgy as derived from and leading to a richer spiritual life, we may well be guilty of fostering an empty ritualism—which is certainly the farthest thing from the kind of liturgical reform that Vatican II invited. One of the main themes that the pioneers who worked toward the renewal of the liturgy in this century stressed was that the liturgy needed to be restored as the prayer and work of the people. In fact, it was Pius X who argued that the reform of the liturgy was crucial to serve the renewal of the church in order, as his motto said, "to restore all things in Christ." One aspect of this needed reform concerned the revision of devotions. The Liturgy Constitution (n. 13) urges that popular devotions be revised so that they would be in accord with the sacred liturgy and the liturgical seasons. This meant, for example, that the balance of praise and petition that the liturgy preserves would be observed in popular devotions as well. It also implied that the kind of theological balance and precision to be found in the revised liturgical rites would then in turn influence the theological balance which popular devotions should maintain, given the fact that the Liturgy Constitution required that devotions be revised to be in harmony with the liturgy.

The Liturgy Constitution also states that the spiritual life "is not limited solely to participation in the liturgy" (n.12), but that other kinds of prayer are required for Christians. I like to illustrate this relationship of the liturgy (as central and pivotal) to other acts of prayer and devotion and to living the spiritual life itself by using three concentric circles (similar to the target for the game of darts or aiming an arrow at a bull's-eye). In this illustration the central circle is *liturgy*. It is in the center because it is, according to the Liturgy Constitution, "the summit toward which the activity of the Church is directed; at the same time it is the font from which the Church's power flows" (n. 10). After all, the liturgy comprises the rites, prayers and ceremonies that are held in common by the whole church throughout the world. The liturgy also comprises all the aspects of our lives before God, from sacramental initiation through the rites of dying and death. Also, the liturgy includes the daily celebration of the Liturgy of the Hours as well as occasional services such as religious profession and other such rites. It is the key, the hinge, the central focus of all of the spiritual life. But clearly the spiritual life is larger than the process of taking part in rites—it involves *life* itself. So, for me, the next of the circles would be labeled *prayer*. The fact that it is a circle that surrounds *liturgy* is one way of illustrating that indeed the liturgy itself is always a prayer. But the fact that this circle is wider than liturgy is meant to indicate that Christians are to engage in other acts of prayer and devotion—not just the liturgy. And when we look (proudly) at our Catholic tradition I think we can justifiably say that the many schools of prayer (monastic, mendicant, apostolic and so forth) all reflect the Catholic genius of emphasizing that prayer is crucial, but that there are a number of ways to express that value.

The final, largest and widest circle, is labeled *spirituality*. This is the largest because, for me, the living of the Christian life as converted and committed people is the chief aim of all our prayer, devotions and pious exercises, including the liturgy. The aim of the liturgy in this sense is to reflect what we celebrate in living the spiritual life with one another before and in the world. This draws out what I have already hinted at—namely that the real purpose of reforming the rites of the Mass is to help us appreciate what we celebrate in it and to help us live what we celebrate in our daily lives. In a sense, it is crucial to underscore that at Mass the bread and wine become the body and blood of Christ so that we who share in these gifts at communion can be the more adequate representatives and reflections of Christ before the world as members of the body of Christ. In this sense there is always the challenge dimension of every act of liturgy. We are always directed to live what we celebrate, to reflect what we celebrate ritually in the way we relate to each other and witness to God's love in the world.

Spirituality is also the largest of the circles and "contains" prayer and liturgy in the sense that spirituality depends on prayer and liturgy for it to be authentic, Christian, theological and other-directed. This is critical, I would argue, especially today, because of a lot that passes for contemporary spirituality. The delusion may well be that New-Age crystals, the seemingly omnipresent representations of angels and the plethora of self-help and advice guidebooks on the best-sellers' lists today may well be self-delusional. I say this because Catholic spirituality always requires a liturgical, prayer component and always implies an other-directed, self-sacrificing and service-oriented component. Catholic spirituality needs liturgy as its mainstay and anchor; it requires that we pray communally and privately to God through Christ in the power of the Holy Spirit in intercession for and with the wider church. And Catholic spirituality in its best stripe always requires that we love and serve others, not just those in our intimate circle of family and friends, or those with whom we agree. Catholic spirituality demands that we imitate Jesus in washing one another's feet, in helping to carry others' crosses and in sharing others' burdens.

In an era that prizes the *self*, this is certainly nothing short of a clear, countercultural challenge. But to be true to our faith and our tradition's understanding of liturgy, prayer and spirituality, we can and may do no other. In a sense this makes liturgy—true liturgy, not just rubrics and rites—nothing short of subversive of the status quo and very challenging to the way things are. But then again, Jesus' dining habits in the gospels were equally subversive and challenging. Therefore we can do and be no other.

101. I hear a lot these days about linking the Eucharist and issues of justice. Can you help me understand why these are so interrelated?

Your question is very contemporary and yet recalls a very traditional theme of our faith and our liturgy. The restoration of the words "justice" and "peace" to our Catholic vocabulary are the direct result of the initiatives at Vatican II and since then in the church teaching, leadership and structure. For example, after Vatican II Pope Paul VI established the Pontifical Council on Justice and Peace as a permanent feature of the church's institutional offices in Rome and the issue of global justice occupied the Synod of Bishops in 1971. That liturgy and justice should be so linked today is a notable and significant revival of part of what I argued in response to the previous question, namely, that liturgy always has implications for human life and that our participation in liturgy should lead to ever deeper participation in living holy and just lives before God in service to others.

Among the notable aspects of reuniting liturgy and justice is that the very notion of *justice* requires that we leave behind any domestic, overly intimate or familial notions of what liturgy is all about. When we use the term "justice," we are immediately directed toward the whole gamut of the way the world limits true justice, particularly in terms of class divisions, tribal conflicts, color or gender discrimination and other such factors. When all of that is in the forefront of our celebration of liturgy, then the widest lens possible is applied to what liturgy should focus on—concerns that are nothing short of global.

At the same time, when we speak of liturgy and justice we are immediately concerned with the fact that what we celebrate is the challenge and gift of *God's* justice. This means that any notions of what justice is derive from the gospels, and these often overturn human expectations in favor of what God has in store for us. This means laying ourselves open to the challenge of paradoxical parables that advocate giving the same wage to all who work in the vineyard no matter the number of hours

(Mt 20:1–16) or the parables proper to Luke about the lost sheep, the lost coin and the prodigal son (Lk 15). In each of these, human logic and our native sense of distributive "justice" are overturned in favor of the overwhelming kindness and amazing grace of God. It is this kind of justice that should be the measure of the world's and the church's expectations, but so often it is not. All too often, we fall back into something akin to what is really condemned in the gospels—an eye for an eye and a tooth for a tooth—whereas God's justice measures out mercy, not condemnation; grace, not judgment. So, in this sense it is most helpful that justice and liturgy have been reunited. Hopefully, this will mean that God's often confounding, always liberating power will break through these rites and ceremonies so that what we experience is an ever more complete identification with God through Christ. It is, after all, he whom we invoke during Advent when we cry, "Let the clouds rain down the Just One." And it is his paschal dying and rising that we take part in (participate in) each time we celebrate the Mass, from which we are sent forth "to love and serve the Lord."